Louisiana Child Custody, Visitation and Child Support Guide

WINNING STEPS FOR YOUR CHILD CUSTODY AND CHILD SUPPORT CASE IN LOUISIANA

(With more specifics about a case in Orleans (New Orleans), Jefferson, St. Tammany, St. Charles, St. John the Baptist, St. Bernard and Plaquemines Parishes)

By
Stephen Rue
Attorney at Law

Voted the "Best Attorney"* and "Best Divorce Lawyer"** In New Orleans*

* *GambitWeekly* Readers Poll, 2013
**<u>*GambitWeekly*</u> Readers Poll, 2002 and 2003

www.RueDivorce.com
StephenRue@me.com
(504) 529-5000

DEDICATION

The Louisiana Child Custody, Visitation, and Child Support Guide is dedicated to the thousands of clients that I have represented over the last twenty five years. I continue to devote my efforts, skill, and professionalism to you and your children. If you would like to schedule an appointment with me, please call my law office at (504) 529-5000.

Additionally, this Guide is dedicated to the children of Louisiana. Through this book, I pray that any parent using this guide will gain knowledge and wisdom to be the best parent that they can be through the custody and child support process and through the rest of your lives.

ACKNOWLEDGEMENTS

I wish to thank my entire team of divorce professionals for their aggressive and professional representation of our clients throughout Louisiana.

PREFACE

The use of The Louisiana Child Custody, Visitation, and Child Support Guide is a very important tool created to assist you in understanding, coping, and managing your life in the context of Louisiana laws regarding the issues of child custody, visitation and child support. The content of this book is predominantly taken from my larger book Louisiana Divorce Handbook which addresses many other issues. This guide is designed to assist those people who need assistance with the specific legal issues of child custody, visitation and child support in Louisiana.

Once you are faced with the realities of an impending divorce, you often don't have the time to read several books regarding the intricate details of divorce litigation. This book is not meant to replace a competent divorce lawyer licensed in Louisiana; however, it will be your quick and concise guide to provide you with the key concepts and knowledge necessary to defeat the normal feelings of overwhelm and despair. You will be able to promptly target your particular concerns and be directed on how to take action to protect your precious rights. Once you have obtained a comfort level with the basic principles of your concerns, this guide will provide further references to assist you with a productive dialogue with your chosen attorney.

Each of the fifty states has unique characteristics in their laws; Louisiana is no different. Of the thousands of clients who have come into one of our law offices in Louisiana, at least half of these clients have concerns about the strange laws of Louisiana and most have heard antiquated vestiges that linger from the obscure "Napoleonic Code." This Louisiana Child Custody, Visitation, and Child Support Guide will provide you an overview of Louisiana family law and explain the most common areas of concerns. With the assistance of your family lawyer, you should have a very good grasp on what to expect and how to optimize favorable results. Each case can only be properly analyzed after considering your particular circumstances and needs. I have worked diligently to provide the most recent facts as they pertain to Louisiana law and the interplay with laws of other states as well as federal legislation; however, the law is dynamic and laws do change. Your lawyer should be able to advise you as to Louisiana's current law and how it relates to you your case. I strongly recommend that you seek professional advice and do not handle your divorce without a lawyer. You may wish to consider consulting an attorney, accountant, certified financial planner, tax advisor, and other such professionals. Discuss the concepts disclosed in this book with your lawyer and consider his advice on each of the issues presented.

In this guide, I will provide helpful gems gathered through representing thousands of clients. Although these gems should not be taken as legal advice, you can gather comfort from knowing that thousands have benefited from understanding the foundation of Louisiana family law and lessons gleamed from my representation of many clients who have found themselves in similar positions. I also have supplied antidotes and illustrative quotes from various clients. Names and localities may have been changed to maintain confidentiality. The purpose of these antidotes and quotes is to let you know that your experience is not uncommon and you will survive the process.

Although selected Louisiana laws are provided, I recommend that you simply read them at your leisure as supplemental information and don't worry about the intricacies of interpretation of these laws. This guide provides you with practical applications of facts that will help you in understanding the process and assisting your selected attorney in the best presentation of your legal interests. If you need further advice, please do not hesitate to contact me.

Extra space is purposefully provided throughout this book so you can place your own notes. Good luck!

THE FOLLOWING ARE YOUR <u>CRITICAL STEPS</u> TO HELP YOU WIN YOUR CHILD CUSTODY AND CHILD SUPPORT CASE IN LOUISIANA!

Attorney-at-Law

TABLE OF CONTENTS

CHAPTER 1

WHAT TO EXPECT

I like being very straight forward with my clients. I always inform them of what to expect while they are going through a divorce, custody or child support proceeding. Simply put, getting a divorce, going through a custody or child support dispute can be a very emotional experience. <u>Expect stress - it is very normal</u>.

Divorce brings concerns about children, money, property, and being single again. There are no Louisiana laws that directly address the emotional stress associated with the divorce process. Although temporary restraining orders and injunctions can eliminate stress and anxiety regarding potentially volatile confrontations with your spouse.

We should not allow our emotions to guide us to act and make decisions that are irrational and that are not in the best interests of our children and ourselves.

EMOTIONS WILL ARISE

Realize that sad emotions will arise. Transcend and separate your emotions from the decisions that affect your finances and your children. The more that emotion becomes involved in your divorce proceeding, the more your divorce process will likely last and cost. As you start to take control of your emotions, you also will start to gain control of your divorce proceeding. Regain inner peace and enjoy your new life. One step towards peacefulness is in knowing what you may encounter in your litigation. This guide will provide you a framework for your expectations.

You may encounter a series of emotions that many refer to the emotional lifecycle of a divorce proceeding.

NORMAL EMOTIONAL LIFE CYCLE
OF A DIVORCE

> Denial or Surprise

> Anger

> Depression and feelings of despair

> Desires to negotiate with your spouse

> Sadness

> Acceptance and understanding

> Pursuit for further happiness

YOU ARE NOT ALONE
AND YOUR EXPERIENCE IS NOT UNIQUE

Each year <u>over two million people</u> divorce, and fight over custody and child support. Remember that each year over two million people divorce and encounter some form of anxiety, doubt, denial, depression, loneliness, guilt, anger, sadness, feelings that overwhelm, forgetfulness, and/or frustration. They also may feel a sense of relief. It is unlikely that you will be able to avoid these pressures. What you can control is your body and your mind. Remember that divorce no longer carries a stigma of shame.

You are not the honoree at a Louisiana jazz funeral - you are getting divorced - Life goes on!

DIVORCE STATISTICS

We have all heard that the divorce rate is at an alarming fifty (50%) percent of marriages. Society is beginning to look at marriage as a contract. As a result of this sterile view of the union, judges are becoming more dispassionate towards particular litigants. Today many have considered that a divorce is like going to the dentist and getting a tooth pulled. It may be painful, but it also can be quick.

Approximately 95% of divorce proceedings do not result in a contested trial. (Source: American Bar Association) Each year, approximately two million people get divorced. The divorce rate hovers around 4.4 to 4.6 divorces per every 1,000 in population. In the seventies and eighties, the divorce rate climbed from 2.5/1000 in 1966 to highs of 5.3/1000 in 1979 and 1981. The divorce rate has leveled off since the 1981 peak.

The average length of a first marriage is 11 years. A woman remarries for an average of 7.1 years, while men remarry for an average of 7.4 years. The average duration of an American marriage is 9.8 years. The average age for a woman who marries and divorces several times is 33 for the first divorce, 39 for the second, and 42 for three or more. The average age for men of multiple divorces is 35 for the first, 42 for the second, and 46.5 for subsequent divorces.

Divorces are more prevalent during the time when men are, on average, 30–34 years old and for women 25–29 years old. A female's divorce rate is highest between the very young ages of 15 and 19. A male's divorce rate is highest between the ages of 20 and 24.

At the time of their first marriage, the median age for women is 21.0 years and 23.1 years for men. The median age of spouses at the time of the first marriage divorce decree is 35.1 for women and 33.2 for men.

Women start the legal proceedings in more than 90 percent of all divorces.

YOUR OWN EMOTIONAL AND PHYSICAL WELL BEING AFFECTS YOUR CHANCES OF GETTING CUSTODY OR VISITATION OF YOUR CHILDREN

LA C.C. Art. 134. Lists the factors that are used to determine the child's best interest for custody and visitation decisions. Two of the factors directly involve your physical and emotional well-being.

The court shall consider all relevant factors in determining the best interest of the child. Such factors may include:

(1) The love, affection, and other emotional ties between each party and the child....(7) The mental and physical health of each party.
Art 134 stated in pertinent part.

Art. 136. addresses an award of visitation rights to a parent and considers
(4) The willingness of the relative to encourage a close relationship between the child and his parent or parents.
and (5) The mental and physical health of the child and the relative.
Art 136, stated in pertinent part.

GOOD TO YOURSELF

Celebrate each day in your life. Take good care of yourself. Eating healthy and exercising regularly will allow you to be physically and mentally prepared for this time of inherent stress and uncertainty. Anger and bitterness eat at you if you let them. The person most hurt by your rage is you. Don't forget, don't regress, but do forgive your spouse for your own sake, and for the sake of your children. This is not to say that you should forgive and reconcile, but rather, forgive for the sake of being happy. Forgive for the sake of being healthy. Forgive for the sake of moving on. Get what is just and fair to you and the children. Forgive and live. If you feel overwhelmed, consider seeking advice from a mental health professional and/or religious and spiritual advisor. Also seek help for any substance abuse problem. Remember that your lawyer is not a therapist. Other professionals are better equipped to handle your emotional needs. If time permits, reading books regarding divorce and related issues also will reduce your level of stress.

- It's O.K. to cry and express your feelings.

- Talk to <u>supportive</u> friends that do not flame the fire of your anger or grief.

- Read books that help you get through the divorce process.

- Consider joining a divorce support group.

- Exercise regularly.

- Eat healthy.

- Resist destructive temptations

- Consult a counselor or religious advisor.

- Focus on your career or potential career

TALK TO YOUR CHILDREN

Take time to talk with your children and explain that you are getting a divorce. Tailor your statements to the age of the children. Emphasize that the break up is not their fault and that your decision to divorce is made and that they cannot change it. Do not speak badly of the other parent. Frequently reassure the children that both of you are still their parents and that they are loved and will not be abandoned. Tell them that you will take care of them and keep them safe. Everything will be all right!

SUMMARY OF TIPS TO HELP
CONTROL YOUR BODY AND MIND

1. Remember that you are not alone.
2. Eat Healthy.
3. Exercise Regularly.
4. Seek help for any substance abuse that you may have.
5. Resist destructive temptations.
6. It's O.K. to cry and express your feelings.
7. Talk to <u>supportive</u> friends that do not flame the fire of your anger or grief.
8. Consider joining a divorce support group.
9. Consult a counselor or religious advisor.
10. Focus on your career or potential career
11. Read books about divorce and related issues.
12. Remember that your lawyer is not trained to be a psychiatrist, use the lawyer for your legal problems.
13. Talk to your children and let them know that they are loved, not abandoned, and that the break up is not their fault.
14. Forgive and live. Remember the emotional lifecycle of a divorce.
15. Be Happy.

CHAPTER 2

GET POSSESSION OF CHILDREN AND PROPERTY

GET POSSESSION

In a divorce case, possession of children and property is everything. Get and keep the physical custody of your children, money, documents, and property. Safeguard everyone and everything. You must protect your monetary assets during a divorce. You and your spouse have conflicting financial interests.

CHILDREN

Without a court order indicating which parent has temporary physical custody of your children, both parents have equal rights to the children. If you want custody of your children, go get your children. If you have possession of your children, keep them. Immediately have your attorney file a motion asking for the temporary custody of your children and a restraining order preventing your spouse from taking them without your written permission.

LA-C.C. Art. 131 Court to determine custody

In a proceeding for divorce or thereafter, the court shall award custody of a child in accordance with the best interest of the child.

LA-C.C. Art. 132 Award of custody to parents

If the parents agree who is to have custody, the court shall award custody in accordance with their agreement unless the best interest of the child requires a different award.

In the absence of agreement, or if the agreement is not in the best interest of the child, the court shall award custody to the parents jointly; however, if custody in one parent is shown by clear and convincing evidence to serve the best interest of the child, the court shall award custody to that parent.

LA-C.C.P. Art. 3945. Incidental order of temporary child custody; injunctive relief; exceptions
A. The injunctive relief afforded either party to an action for divorce or other proceeding which includes a provision for the temporary custody of a minor child shall be governed by the additional provisions of this Article.

B. An ex parte order of temporary custody of a minor child shall not be granted unless:

(1) It clearly appears from specific facts shown by a verified petition or by supporting affidavit that immediate and irreparable injury will result to the child before the adverse party or his attorney can be heard in opposition.

(2) The applicant's attorney certifies to the court, in writing, either:

(a) The efforts which have been made to give the adverse party reasonable notice of the date and time such order is being presented to the court.

(b) The reasons supporting his claim that notice should not be required.

C. An ex parte order of temporary custody shall:

(1) Expire by operation of law within fifteen days of signing of the order; however, the order may be extended for good cause shown at any time before its expiration for one period not exceeding ten days.

(2) Provide specific provisions for temporary visitation by the adverse party of not less than forty-eight hours during the fifteen-day period, unless the

verified petition or supporting affidavit clearly demonstrates that immediate and irreparable injury will result to the child as a result of such visitation.

(3) Be endorsed with the date on which the ex parte order is signed and the date and hour of the rule to show cause.

D. The rule to show cause why the respondent should not be awarded the custody, joint custody, or visitation of the child shall be assigned for hearing not more than fifteen days after signing of the ex parte order of temporary custody.

E. Any ex parte order not in compliance with the provisions of this Article is not enforceable, and is null and void.

F. In the event an ex parte order of temporary custody is denied, the court shall specifically allocate between the parents the time which the child shall spend with each parent, unless immediate and irreparable injury will result to the child.

G. The provisions of this Article do not apply to any order of custody of a child requested in a verified petition alleging the applicability of the Domestic Abuse Assistance Act, R.S. 46:2131 et seq., Children's Code Article 1564 et seq., or the Post-Separation Family Violence Relief Act, R.S. 9:361 et seq.

PETS

Despite popular sentiment, in Louisiana pets are "property." If you want your pets, keep them. When you hire an attorney, tell him of your concerns regarding your pets. The facts regarding how you acquired them are very important.

MONEY

Get cash from all available sources. Make sure enough money is kept in accounts to pay for previously written checks. Also speak to your attorney, CPA, and certified financial planner about other legal, tax and financial consequences.

THE HOUSE/APARTMENT/FURNISHINGS

If you want possession of your house or apartment, remain there. If you are battered or otherwise abused, immediately seek assistance.

LA-R.S. 9:374 Possession and use of family residence or community movables or immovables

A. When the family residence is the separate property of either spouse, after the filing of a petition for divorce or in conjunction therewith, the spouse who has physical custody or has been awarded temporary custody of the minor children of the marriage may petition for, and a court may award to that spouse, after a contradictory hearing, the use and occupancy of the family residence pending the partition of the community property or one hundred eighty days after termination of the marriage, whichever occurs first. In these cases, the court shall inquire into the relative economic status of the spouses, including both community and separate property, and the needs of the children, and shall award the use and occupancy of the family residence to the spouse in accordance with the best interest of the family. The court shall consider the granting of the occupancy of the family home in awarding spousal support.

B. When the family residence is community property or the spouses own community movables or immovables, after or in conjunction with the filing of a petition for divorce or for separation of property in accordance with Civil Code Article 2374, either spouse may petition for, and a court may award to one of the spouses, after a contradictory hearing, the use and occupancy of the family residence and use of community movables or immovables to either of the spouses pending further order of the court. In these cases, the court shall inquire into the relative economic status of the spouses, including both community and separate property, and the needs of the children, if any, and shall award the use and occupancy of the family residence and the use of any community movables or immovables to the spouse in accordance with the best interest of the family. If applicable, the court shall consider the granting of the occupancy of the family home and the use of community movables or immovables in awarding spousal support.

C. A spouse who uses and occupies or is awarded by the court the use and occupancy of the family residence pending either the termination of the marriage or the partition of the community property in accordance with the provisions of R.S. 9:374(A) or (B) shall not be liable to the other spouse for rental for the use and occupancy, unless otherwise agreed by the spouses or ordered by the court.

D. The court may determine whether the family home is separate or community property in the contradictory hearing authorized under the provisions of this Section.

E. (1) In a proceeding for divorce or thereafter, upon request of either party, where a community property regime existed, a summary proceeding may be undertaken by the trial court within sixty days of filing, allocating the use of community property, including monetary assets, bank accounts, savings plans, and other divisible movable property pending formal partition proceeding, pursuant to R.S. 9:2801.

(2) Upon court order, each spouse shall provide the other a complete accounting of all community assets subsequent to said allocation and in compliance with Civil Code Article 2369.3, providing the duty to preserve and prudently manage community

property.

(3) The court shall determine allocation of community assets after considering:

(a) The custody of the children and exclusive possession of the house.
(b) The total community assets.
(c) The need of one spouse for funds to maintain a household prior to formal partition.
(d) The need of a spouse to receive legal representation during the course of the divorce proceeding.

BE THE QUEEN OR KING OF THE CASTLE

After consulting with your attorney, consider changing the locks of your house or apartment. Be sure to get the approval of your lawyer because in many states, to prohibit a spouse from entering their own house/apartment without a court order, may be considered "constructive abandonment."

DON'T GET LOCKED OUT OF YOUR HOUSE/APARTMENT

If your spouse changes the locks at your house or apartment, immediately call your attorney, your spouse, and the police to see if your spouse has a legal right to prohibit you from being in your house/apartment.

Ask your lawyer to file a motion seeking a restraining order against your spouse from locking you out of your residence.

INVENTORY EVERYTHING

You can prevent trying to rely solely on your memory by inventorying your property. Once you have a good inventory of these items, consider photographing and/or videotaping them. Additionally, get a friend to view all of the items and provide the date and his initials next to each item that he inspects so that he later may testify as a witness as to the existence and condition of your property, should the property disappear.

When listing all of your financial records, including credit card accounts, car titles, and insurance policies, be sure to be as specific as possible by including the account number and account balances at the time that you make your list. Get the originals or copies of all documents.

You may use the forms found in the Appendix to assist you in this inventory process. As an additional mental reminder, use the following list to assist you in your quest to locate, inventory, possess, and/or photocopy.

DOCUMENTS AND THINGS TO
LOCATE, INVENTORY, POSSESS, AND/OR COPY

Gather documents and things regarding you, your spouse and your children as to the following:

Income Information:
- Pay checks
- Payroll stubs
- Federal and state income tax returns and refunds
- Cash register receipts
- Receipt records
- Deferred, retirement, and/or savings plans such as IRAs, 401Ks, profit sharing, and stock options
- Severance pay
- "Golden parachute" retirement plans
- Documents evidencing any company or employer reimbursement for entertainment, travel, automobile, and/or other expenses
- Other employment benefits such as sick pay, vacation pay, bonuses, health club and country club memberships, and frequent flier programs
- Financial statements, balance sheets, profit and loss statements, and income statements
- Records regarding rental income
- Bank accounts: checking, savings, money market, and line of credit   accounts
- Scholastic and vocational diplomas, awards, and/or degrees

Investment Information:
- Stocks, bonds, mutual funds, promissory notes, options, certificates of deposit, purchase agreements, and other investments

- All financial statements
- Trust agreements
- Custodial accounts

Bank Records:
- Checkbook registers
- Canceled checks
- Savings accounts
- Christmas club accounts
- Loan applications
- Documents in safety deposit boxes
- Insurance Information:
- Insurance policies, whether life, health, auto, disability, or other.

Cars, Boats, Motorcycles, Motor Homes, Trailers, and Airplanes:
- Titles and registrations
- Keys
- Actual vehicles
- Appraisals on all vehicles

Marriage Related Documents:
- Present and prior marriage licenses, divorce papers, adoption papers
- Inheritance documents, judgments regarding child support
- Prenuptial, ante nuptial agreements

Real Estate and Furniture:
- Titles or deeds to all property
- Appraisals of property
- Evaluations of furniture, furnishings, etc.
- Time-share unit's agreements
- Household furniture and furnishings

Other Business Records:

- Articles of incorporation, initial and annual reports, minute books, stockholder subscriptions, partnership agreements, and other documentation concerning the financial condition of any legal entity in which your spouse has or had a legal or equitable interest

Medical Records:
- Medical records
- Counseling and/or psychological evaluations of any party to this litigation and/or of the minor child
- Medical insurance cards
- Dental and orthodontic records
- Prescriptions

Other Monthly Expenses:
- All current invoices/bills
- Housing (Rent or mortgage note payment)
- Property insurance and taxes
- Premises/yard maintenance and repair
- Condominium charges
- Furniture payments
- Household supplies and repairs
- Utilities
- Electricity
- Gas
- Water
- Telephone
- Home
- Car
- Beeper
- Cable
- Food
- Groceries
- Meals eaten out/including work lunches
- Automobile/Transportation

- Car note
- Gasoline
- Car maintenance
- Parking
- Other transportation expenses
- Clothing
- Average new purchases/replacements
- Dry cleaning and laundry
- Personal and grooming (haircuts/nails)
- Education
- School/lessons/tutoring
- Books
- Miscellaneous education expenses
- Day-care/baby sitting
- Pet/pet supplies
- Maid
- Union dues
- Recreation
- Gifts, donations, religious tithes
- Vacation
- Other debts

Miscellaneous Documents and Things:
- Pets
- Jewelry
- Artwork
- Antiques and collectibles
- Birth certificates
- Passports/Visas/Green cards
- Vaccination records

YOUR FINANCIAL FIGURES ARE YOUR FRIENDS

If your spouse is not anticipating your move towards a divorce, then methodically and discreetly get originals or copies of all financial records regarding your spouse's business affairs and income as well as both of your expenses. Safeguard these documents with your attorney, a confidant, or in a new safety deposit box at a new bank.

GET INFORMATION FROM COMPUTERS

Make a backup tape or diskette of the information on your computer. Give the tape and or diskette to your attorney. Also consider making a print out of any particularly revealing data.

10. GET POSSESSION OF ALL DOCUMENTS THAT YOU NEED TO PREPARE YOUR TAXES

Accumulate all documents that you will need to prepare your taxes.

VIDEOTAPE AND/OR PHOTOGRAPH EACH ROOM OF YOUR HOUSE/APARTMENT

FILE "EX PARTE" MOTIONS

Often the test on who gets the immediate possession of children, money, homes, and property, depends on who wins the race to the courthouse and files "Ex Parte" motions. These pleadings permit you to get the possession of children and things or injunctions under certain circumstances without an initial court hearing. Talk to your attorney about what circumstances may apply for you.

LA-C.C.P. Art. 3601 Injunction, grounds for issuance; preliminary injunction; temporary restraining order

An injunction shall issue in cases where irreparable injury, loss, or damage may otherwise result to the applicant, or in other cases specifically provided by law; provided, however, that no court shall have jurisdiction to issue, or cause to be issued, any temporary restraining order, preliminary injunction, or permanent injunction against any state department, board or agency, or any officer, administrator or head thereof, or any officer of the State of Louisiana in any suit involving the expenditure of public funds under any statute or law of this state to compel the expenditure of state funds when the director of such department, board or agency, or the governor shall certify that the expenditure of such funds would have the effect of creating a deficit in the funds of said agency or be in violation of the requirements placed upon the expenditure of such funds by the legislature.

During the pendency of an action for an injunction the court may issue a temporary restraining order, a preliminary injunction, or both, except in cases where prohibited, in accordance with the provisions of this Chapter.

Except as otherwise provided by law, an application for injunctive relief shall be by petition.

CHAPTER 3

PATERNITY

A prerequisite to the establishment of child custody or support is the determination of paternity and maternity. In most cases, the matter is not disputed and both parents have their names on the child's birth certificate. However, in a growing number of cases, the paternity of the child is in dispute. The majority of the time, the biological mother is trying to prove that a certain man is the biological father of a child. In other instances, the presumed father is in doubt of his paternity because of reservations about the mother's fidelity. Regardless of the reason, the matter may come into dispute. When it does, the Louisiana legislature and courts have created a body of law and testing procedures to deal with these concerns.

TIME IS OF THE ESSENCE WHEN ESTABLISHING OR DISAVOWING PATERNITY

Whether you wish to establish or disavow paternity, the time allowed to bring the matter before a court is passing (it may have already passed). Immediately seek your attorney's assistance if paternity or maternity is at issue.

LOUISIANA CLASSIFICATIONS OF CHILDREN

1. Legitimate

2. Illegitimate

In Louisiana, children are either legitimate or illegitimate. (LCC Art. 178) Legitimate children are those who are either born or conceived during marriage or who have been legitimated as provided hereafter. (LCC Art. 179) Illegitimate children are those who are conceived and born out of marriage. (LCC Art. 180) The classification of illegitimate children may be changed to legitimate through legal proceedings. (LRS Art. 9: 46 and 9:391)

LOUISIANA'S LAWS OF PRESUMPTION OF PATERNITY

Most states, including Louisiana, have enacted laws that provide that if a couple is married during the conception or birth of a child, then the couple is "presumed" to be the biological parents of the child. Since the chief goal of these laws is to establish paternity, Louisiana addresses this issue in terms of the "husband" being the "father" of the child. The Louisiana law provides a "rebut table presumption" in which the parent can go to court, within a limited time period, and attempt to prove that he is not the parent of the child.

Other states have a more narrow stance on paternity/maternity. These state laws provide that if a couple is married during the conception or birth of a child, then it is "conclusive" that the couple are the parents of the child.

Whether "rebut table presumptions" or "conclusive presumptions" exist, the states have taken the parental policy of making it difficult to make a child illegitimate.

In Louisiana, if a couple is not married, no presumption regarding paternity is applicable.

THE HUSBAND IS PRESUMED TO BE THE FATHER; THE PRESUMPTION IS REBUTTABLE

> **LA-C.C. Art. 184. Presumed paternity of husband**
>
> The husband of the mother is presumed to be the father of all children born or conceived during the marriage.

The husband of the mother is presumed to be the father of all children born or conceived during the marriage. (LCC Art. 184) Additionally a child born less than three hundred days after the dissolution of the marriage is presumed to have been conceived during the marriage. A child born three hundred days or more after the dissolution of the marriage is not presumed to be the child of the husband. (LCC Art. 185)

> **LA-C.C. Art. 185 . Presumption of paternity, date of birth**
>
> A child born less than three hundred days after the dissolution of the marriage is presumed to have been conceived during the marriage. A child born three hundred days or more after the dissolution of the marriage is not presumed to be the child of the husband

The husband of the mother is not presumed to be the father of the child if another man is presumed to be the father. (LCC Art. 186)

A MOTHER'S PROOF OF PATERNITY

1. Birth certificate (LCC Art. 193)
2. Evidence of reputation that the child has been consistently considered as a child born during the marriage (LCC Art. 194)
3. Evidence of reputation sufficient to establish material facts such as:
a. That such individual has always been called by the surname of the father from whom he pretends to be born;
b. That the father treated him as his child, and that he provided as such for his education, maintenance and settlement in life;
c. That he has constantly been acknowledged as such in the world;
d. That he has been acknowledged as such within the family. (LCC Art. 195)
4. Written or oral evidence (LCC Art. 196)
5. Formal or informal acknowledgement of child before or after marriage to the mother (LCC Art. 198)
6. The alleged father's signature on a notarized act of acknowledgment (LCC Art. 200)
7. Evidence of hospital bills. (LRS Art. 9:394)
8. Genetic testing –DNA (LRS Art. 9:394)
9. Blood Sample (LRS Art. 398.2)
10. Father's written act of acknowledgement (LCC Art. 110 and LRS 9:392)

GENETIC TESTING (DNA) IS THE MOTHER OF ALL PROOF

> **LA-R.S. 9:394 Evidence of hospital bills and tests in paternity action**
>
> In an action to establish paternity, originals or certified copies of bills for pregnancy, childbirth, and genetic testing shall be admissible as an exception to the hearsay rule and shall be prima facie evidence that the amounts reflected on the bills were incurred for such services or testing on behalf of the child. Extrinsic evidence of authenticity of the bills, or their duplicates, as a condition precedent to admissibility shall not be required.

Science has advanced to a point where most of the guess work is taken out of a paternity dispute. Genetic DNA testing has become the norm for disputed paternity cases. Each state has established a "threshold" (percentage requirement) for genetic test results in which a rebut table or conclusive presumption of paternity is created if the probability of paternity is equal to or greater than a threshold percentage (i.e., alleged father's probability of being the child's biological father is a 99% likelihood according to DNA test results).

DNA testing can be accomplished as early as nine to ten weeks of pregnancy. Tests can be taken of the fetus through chronic villis sampling (CVS). Although rarely used, this technique is available and may be valuable in assisting your attorney in seeking the establishment of paternity at the earliest time allowed by state law.

APPOINTMENT OF AN ATTORNEY TO REPRESENT THE CHILD'S INTEREST IN AN ACTION TO DISAVOW PATERNITY

In any action to disavow paternity, the judge shall appoint an attorney to represent the child whose status is at issue, and the attorney so appointed shall not represent any other party in the litigation. (LCC Art. 5091.1)

A MAN'S ACTION TO DISAVOW

LCC Art. 187 provides the burden of proof necessary for a husband to disavow the paternity of a child.

```
┌─────────────────────────────────────────────┐
│        EVIDENCE OFTEN USED TO DISAVOW         │
│                  PATERNITY:                   │
│                                               │
│  1. Negative blood tests.                     │
│  2. Unmatched DNA prints.                     │
│  3. Sterility.                                │
│  4. Physical impossibility because of location during │
│     the time of conception.                   │
│  5. Any other scientific or medical evidence which │
│     the court may deem relevant under the     │
│     circumstances.                            │
└─────────────────────────────────────────────┘
```

A husband may loose his right to disavow paternity. A man who marries a pregnant woman and who knows that she is pregnant at the time of the marriage cannot disavow the paternity of such child born of such pregnancy. However, if the woman has acted in bad faith and has made a false claim of fatherhood to the marrying spouse, he may disavow paternity provided that he proves such bad faith on the part of the mother, and he proves by a preponderance of the evidence that the child is not his. If another man is presumed to be the father, however, then the provisions of Article 186 apply. The husband also cannot disavow paternity of a child born as the result of artificial insemination of the mother to which he consented. (LCC Art. 188)

THERE IS A TIME LIMIT FOR A HUSBAND TO DISAVOW

One may file a lawsuit to disavow paternity which must be filed within one year after the husband learned or should have learned of the birth of the child; but, if the husband for reasons beyond his control is not able to file suit timely, then the time for filing suit shall be suspended during the period of such inability. Nevertheless, the suit may be filed within one year from the date the husband is notified in writing that a party in interest has asserted that the husband is the father of the child, if the husband lived continuously separate and apart from the mother during the three hundred days immediately preceding the birth of the child. (LCC Art. 189)

LYING UNDER OATH IN A PATERNITY CASE

Whoever intentionally falsely swears in a paternity case may be may be fined up to five hundred dollars, or imprisoned for up to six months, or both. (LRS Art. 9:125.1)

TIME LIMIT TO DISAVOW AND TIME TO ESTABLISH PATERNITY

States have established narrow time limits (usually less than one year from birth) for a father to attempt to legally disavow a child. Again, the policy is intended to prevent the child from becoming legally illegitimate, regardless as to whether the husband is the father. On the other hand, states have established much broader time frames to allow the establishment of paternity. In many states, after a child reaches the "age of majority," he has another one to five years to seek the establishment of paternity.

CHAPTER 4

CHILD CUSTODY AND VISITATION

BEST ADVICE: BE A GOOD PARENT!

Although being a good parent, seems like obvious advice, many parents loose sight of this primary responsibility while in the throws of an emotional and otherwise trying legal custody battle.

Quick Facts:

There are 11.5 million American divorced custodial parents are comprised of 9.9 million women and 1.6 million men (U.S. Census Bureau).

According to national statistics, for each divorce decree granted, an average of one minor child (under the age of 18) is involved (0.9 per divorce decree). Thus, under the current divorce rate, more than one million additional children are directly affected by a divorce each year (1,075,000).

Throughout America, mothers are awarded sole custody of their children 71 percent of the time. Joint custody awards occur 15.5 percent of the time. Fathers receive the sole custody award 8.5 percent of the time.   And friends and other relatives receive custody in 5 percent of all custody decrees.

WHAT IS CUSTODY?

Custody can be defined in terms of physical possession or in terms of legal responsibilities. Custody may be temporary or permanent; joint, shared, or sole; and legal and/or physical.

LEGAL CUSTODY AND PHYSICAL CUSTODY

The heart and soul of "legal custody" is in the ability of a parent to make these crucial decisions regarding the child, including the day to day decisions of child rearing. Physical custody, as the term suggests, is the actual physical possession and control of the child.

LA-C.C. Art. 131 Court to determine custody

In a proceeding for divorce or thereafter, the court shall award custody of a child in accordance with the best interest of the child.

LA-C.C. Art. 132 Award of custody to parents

If the parents agree who is to have custody, the court shall award custody in accordance with their agreement unless the best interest of the child requires a different award.

In the absence of agreement, or if the agreement is not in the best interest of the child, the court shall award custody to the parents jointly; however, if custody in one parent is shown by clear and convincing evidence to serve the best interest of the child, the court shall award custody to that parent.

LA-C.C.P. Art. 3945. Incidental order of temporary child custody; injunctive relief; exceptions

A. The injunctive relief afforded either party to an action for divorce or other proceeding which includes a provision for the temporary custody of a minor child shall be governed by the additional provisions of this Article.

B. An ex parte order of temporary custody of a minor child shall not be granted unless:

(1) It clearly appears from specific facts shown by a verified petition or by supporting affidavit that immediate and irreparable injury will result to the child before the adverse party or his attorney can be heard in opposition.

(2) The applicant's attorney certifies to the court, in writing, either:

(a) The efforts which have been made to give the adverse party reasonable notice of the date and time such order is being presented to the court.

(b) The reasons supporting his claim that notice should not be required.

C. An ex parte order of temporary custody shall:

(1) Expire by operation of law within fifteen days of signing of the order; however, the order may be extended for good cause shown at any time before its expiration for one period not exceeding ten days.

(2) Provide specific provisions for temporary visitation by the adverse party of not less than forty-eight hours during the fifteen-day period, unless the

verified petition or supporting affidavit clearly demonstrates that immediate and irreparable injury will result to the child as a result of such visitation.

(3) Be endorsed with the date on which the ex parte order is signed and the date and hour of the rule to show cause.

D. The rule to show cause why the respondent should not be awarded the custody, joint custody, or visitation of the child shall be assigned for hearing not more than fifteen days after signing of the ex parte order of temporary custody.

E. Any ex parte order not in compliance with the provisions of this Article is not enforceable, and is null and void.

F. In the event an ex parte order of temporary custody is denied, the court shall specifically allocate between the parents the time which the child shall spend with each parent, unless immediate and irreparable injury will result to the child.

G. The provisions of this Article do not apply to any order of custody of a child requested in a verified petition alleging the applicability of the Domestic Abuse Assistance Act, R.S. 46:2131 et seq., Children's Code Article 1564 et seq., or the Post-Separation Family Violence Relief Act, R.S. 9:361 et seq.

TEMPORARY CUSTODY

Temporary custody (also referred to as "Provisional Custody" or "Interim Custody") generally means that the person possessing temporary/provisional custody has legal possession and control of a child until a court rules otherwise or until an event occurs that would trigger a change or termination in custody (i.e., the child reaching the age of majority, the child being emancipated, etc.). The child will live with a particular parent while the court proceedings are under way. Getting temporary custody has great advantages as often temporary custody leads to permanent custody.

PERMANENT CUSTODY

Permanent custody means, as the name suggests, a continued possession and control of a child after the custody matter has been resolved in court or agreed upon by the parties.

JOINT CUSTODY

LA-R.S. 9:335 Joint custody decree and implementation order A. (1) In a proceeding in which joint custody is decreed, the court shall render a joint custody implementation order except for good cause shown.

(2)(a) The implementation order shall allocate the time periods during which each parent shall have physical custody of the child so that the child is assured of frequent and continuing contact with both parents.

(b) To the extent it is feasible and in the best interest of the child, physical custody of the children should be shared equally.

(3) The implementation order shall allocate the legal authority and responsibility of the parents.

B. (1) In a decree of joint custody the court shall designate a domiciliary parent except when there is an implementation order to the contrary or for other good cause shown.

(2) The domiciliary parent is the parent with whom the child shall primarily reside, but the other parent shall have physical custody during time periods that

assure that the child has frequent and continuing contact with both parents.

(3) The domiciliary parent shall have authority to make all decisions affecting the child unless an implementation order provides otherwise. All major decisions made by the domiciliary parent concerning the child shall be subject to review by the court upon motion of the other parent. It shall be presumed that all major decisions made by the domiciliary parent are in the best interest of the child.

C. If a domiciliary parent is not designated in the joint custody decree and an implementation order does not provide otherwise, joint custody confers upon the parents the same rights and responsibilities as are conferred on them by the provisions of Title VII of Book I of the Civil Code.

LA-R.S. 9:336 Obligation of joint custodians to confer

Joint custody obligates the parents to exchange information concerning the health, education, and welfare of the child and to confer with one another in exercising decision-making authority

SHARED CUSTODY

LA-R.S. 9:315.9 Effect of shared custodial arrangement
(1) "Shared custody" means a joint custody order in which each parent has physical custody of the child for an approximately equal amount of time.

(2) If the joint custody order provides for shared custody, the basic child support obligation shall first be multiplied by one and one-half and then divided between the parents in proportion to their respective adjusted gross incomes.

(3) Each parent's theoretical child support obligation shall then be cross multiplied by the actual percentage of time the child spends with the other party to determine the basic child support obligation based on the amount of time spent with the other party.

(4) Each parent's proportionate share of work-related net child care costs and extraordinary adjustments to the schedule shall be added to the amount calculated under Paragraph (3) of this Subsection.

(5) Each parent's proportionate share of any direct payments ordered to be made on behalf of the child for net child care costs, the cost of health insurance premiums, extraordinary medical expenses, or other extraordinary expenses shall be deducted from the amount calculated under Paragraph (3) of this Subsection.

(6) The parent owing the greater amount of child support shall owe to the other parent the difference between the two amounts as a child support obligation. The amount owed shall not be higher than the amount which that parent would have owed if he or she were a domiciliary parent.

B. Worksheet B reproduced in R.S. 9:315.20, or a substantially similar form adopted by local court rule, shall be used to determine child support in accordance with this Subsection.

SPLIT CUSTODY

LA-R.S. 9:315.10 Effect of split custodial arrangement

A. (1) "Split custody" means that each party is the sole custodial or domiciliary parent of at least one child to whom support is due.

(2) If the custody order provides for split custody, each parent shall compute a total child support obligation for the child or children in the custody of the other parent, based on a calculation pursuant to this Section.

(3) The amount determined under Paragraph (2) of this Subsection shall be a theoretical support obligation owed to each parent.

(4) The parent owing the greater amount of child support shall owe to the other parent the difference between the two amounts as a child support obligation.

B. Worksheet A reproduced in R.S. 9:315.20**, or a substantially similar form adopted by local court rule, shall be used by each parent to determine child support in accordance with this Section.**

SOLE CUSTODY

Sole custody is more readily seen in cases where one parent is found to be neglectful, abusive, or mentally/physically incapable of taking care of a child. Sole custody is also found by consent of the parents.

CUSTODY TO A NON-PARENT

LA-C.C. Art. 133 Award of custody to person other than a parent; order of preference

If an award of joint custody or of sole custody to either parent would result in substantial harm to the child, the court shall award custody to another person with whom the child has been living in a wholesome and stable environment, or otherwise to any other person able to provide an adequate and stable environment.

"BEST INTEREST OF CHILD" STANDARD

The ultimate criteria used in determining which parent gets primary custody of a child is the court's evaluation of what is in the "best interest" of the minor child. In general terms, the "best interest" test inquires into the safety, health, happiness, and well-being of the child.

A child's relationship with both parents is very important to the child's future. Children who do not have an active relationship with a parent are more likely to commit crimes, do poorly in school, drop out of school, and have greater psychological health concerns.

LA-C.C. Art. 134 Factors in determining child's best interest

The court shall consider all relevant factors in determining the best interest of the child. Such factors may include:

(1) The love, affection, and other emotional ties between each party and the child.

(2) The capacity and disposition of each party to give the child love, affection, and spiritual guidance and to continue the education and rearing of the child.

(3) The capacity and disposition of each party to provide the child with food, clothing, medical care, and other material needs.

(4) The length of time the child has lived in a stable, adequate environment, and the desirability of maintaining continuity of that environment.

(5) The permanence, as a family unit, of the existing or proposed custodial home or homes.

(6) The moral fitness of each party, insofar as it affects the welfare of the child.

(7) The mental and physical health of each party.

(8) The home, school, and community history of the

child.

(9) The reasonable preference of the child, if the court deems the child to be of sufficient age to express a preference.

(10) The willingness and ability of each party to facilitate and encourage a close and continuing relationship between the child and the other party.

(11) The distance between the respective residences of the parties.

(12) The responsibility for the care and rearing of the child previously exercised by each party.

CLOSED CUSTODY HEARING AVAILABLE

LA-C.C. Art. 135 Closed custody hearing

A custody hearing may be closed to the public.

VISITATION RIGHTS

LA-C.C. Art. 136 Award of visitation rights A. A parent not granted custody or joint custody of a child is entitled to reasonable visitation rights unless the court finds, after a hearing, that visitation would not be in the best interest of the child.

B. Under extraordinary circumstances, a relative, by blood or affinity, or a former stepparent or step-grandparent, not granted custody of the child may be granted reasonable visitation rights if the court finds that it is in the best interest of the child. In determining the best interest of the child, the court shall consider:

(1) The length and quality of the prior relationship between the child and the relative.

(2) Whether the child is in need of guidance, enlightenment, or tutelage which can best be provided by the relative.

(3) The preference of the child if he is determined to be of sufficient maturity to express a preference.

(4) The willingness of the relative to encourage a

close relationship between the child and his parent or parents.

(5) The mental and physical health of the child and the relative.

C. In the event of a conflict between this Article and R.S. 9:344 or 345, the provisions of the statute shall supersede those of this Article.

FACTORS USED IN DETERMINING CUSTODY AND VISITATION RULINGS IN LOUISIANA

States have adopted general guidelines to aid the courts in determining what custody and visitation arrangements are in the "best interest of the children." Louisiana's child custody factors are as follows: The love, affection, and other emotional ties between each party and the child.

1. The capacity and disposition of each party to give the child love, affection, and spiritual guidance and to continue the education and rearing of the child
2. The capacity and disposition of each party to provide the child with food, clothing, medical care, and other material needs
3. The length of time the child has lived in a stable environment, and the desirability of maintaining continuity of that environment
4. The permanence, as a family unit, of the existing

or proposed custodial home or home.
5. The moral fitness of each party, insofar as it affects the welfare of the child
6. The mental and physical health of each party
7. The home, school, and community history of the child
8. The reasonable preference of the child, if the court deems the child to be of sufficient age to express a preference
9. The willingness and ability of each party to facilitate and encourage a close and continuing relationship between the child and the other party
10.   The distance between the respective residences of the parties
11.   The responsibility for the care and rearing of the child previously exercised by each party
Louisiana Civil Code Article 134. (All states have similar provisions.)

Other often unspoken or unconstitutional variables that influence a judge's custody decision include the following:

OTHER FACTORS CONSIDERED:

1. The gender of the child and parent (maternal/paternal preferences)
2. The age of the child and parent
3. The sexual preference of the parent
4. The "significant others" of a parent (i.e., new spouse, boyfriend, girlfriend, other relatives, etc.)
5. The criminal and/or driving record of a parent
6. The race of the child and parent
7. The religious orientation of a parent
8. The temporary custody arrangements currently in effect
9. Keeping children together

10.	The work schedules of the parents
11.	The financial resources of a parent
12.	Alcohol or drug abuse of a parent
13.	History of neglect or abuse and
14.	Which parent lives in the state, county (parish), and city ("Home Cooking!").

YOUR CHILD'S PREFERENCE

One of the most commonly asked questions that lawyers receive in custody disputes is whether the child's preference shall be considered by the judge. There is no set age for a minor child to testify; however, if your child is mature, a judge might allow him to testify in open court or in the judge's chambers.

The judge may consider your child's maturity, intelligence, willingness to testify, his emotional stability, and the child's susceptibility to be bribed or unduly persuaded ("brainwashed").

Children may testify against the "better" parent because of the lack of discipline and rules of the other parent, the bribes of the other parent, the other parent's lies told about you. Children often change their minds on a regular basis. It is not surprising to see that a child tells each parent, in private, that he or she wishes to reside with that parent.

Having the child testify can be very stressful on the child and may lead to psychological problems such as guilt regarding having to choose one parent over the other. You should first ask yourself whether your child should provide any testimony.

As a rule of thumb, most children thirteen (13) or older, will be allowed to testify as to their preferences and any other material facts that he or she has observed. Often a child's preference is revealed to the judge through the report of an evaluator. The child talks to the evaluator and this information is often related to the judge and is often a significant factor in the evaluator's custody recommendation to the court. Usually, children under thirteen (13) years old can tell their preference to the evaluator.

Please be very cautious about bringing your children to court. The event can be very traumatic.

Custodial mothers are more likely than custodial fathers to have never been married. Custodial fathers are more likely to be currently married than their female counterparts; and both parents are equally likely to have been divorced or separated.

Generally, fathers with custody are older than mothers with custody. Approximately 46% of custodial fathers are over forty years old. Only 11% of custodial fathers are 30 years old or younger.

Custodial fathers have more education than the average custodial mother. Men with custody are twice as likely to have a college degree (National Center for Health Statistics).

Children who have fathers that are actively involved in their school lives receive improved grades and are less likely to fail a grade and/or be expelled.

The judge will consider your involvement in the child's life. Do you know all of the following information. If not, get to know these individuals and become very involved in your child's life.

For each child, who is the following person after you in your child's life? What is your relationship with this person? How can you develop a better relationship with that person? Will he or she be a good witness for your custody case? What are the names, addresses, and telephone numbers of the following persons:

IMPORTANT POTENTIAL WITNESSES IN A CUSTODY DISPUTE

☐ Teachers

☐ Day-care providers/baby-sitter/nanny

☐ Coaches

☐ Doctors

☐ Dentist

☐ Priest/pastor/rabbi/spiritual leader

☐ Neighbors

☐ Child's best friends

- Boy scout/cub scout/girl scout/brownie leaders

- School principal

- PTA members

- Sunday school teachers

- Guidance counselor

- Relatives actively involved in child's life

- Other persons actively involved in child's life

- Police officers summoned to any domestic dispute

- Housekeeper

- Psychiatrist/sociologist/social worker

- School nurse

- Instructors of extracurricular activities

FIND OUT WHO IS THE PRIMARY CARETAKER OF YOUR CHILD

An excellent way to assist your attorney and the judge is to establish which parent is actively involved in the day-to-day activities of your child's life. Ask yourself and tell your attorney—who does (or doesn't do) the following tasks:

FACTORS IN DETERMINING WHO IS THE PRIMARY CAREGIVER

- Who wakes up your child?

- Who bathes your child?

- Who grooms your child?

- Who dresses your child?

- Who buys the groceries for your child?

- Who prepares the meals/cooks for your child?

- Who buys your child's clothing?

- Who buys your child's books and uniforms?

- Who takes your child to and from school and/or daycare?

- Who prepares the school lunches for your child?

- Who takes your child to and from extracurricular activities?

- Who coaches or attends the extracurricular activities of your child?

- Who participates in the boy scout or girl scout activities of your child?

- Who attends the PTA meetings?

- Who takes your child to the doctor?

- Who takes your child to the dentist or orthodontist?

- Who keeps the medical records?

- Who stays home from work in order to take care of your sick child?

- Who takes your child to church or synagogue?

- Who takes your child to Sunday school?

- Who assists your child with his or her homework?

- Who attends parent-teacher conferences?

- Who monitors what your child watches on television or at the movies?

- Who changes the diapers?

- Who toilet trains your child?

- Who disciplines your child?

- Who knows your child's friends?

- Who speaks to your child's guidance counselor?

- Who cleans your child's house or bedroom?

- Who cleans your child's clothes?

- Who tucks your child into bed at night?

- Who reads your child bedtime stories?

- Who keeps the house safe for your child?

- Who takes your child to birthday parties?

- Who takes the child "trick or treating"?

- Who regularly communicates with your child?

- Who has custody of any other siblings?

- What else do you do for your child?

KEEP RECEIPTS AND DOCUMENTS REGARDING ALL OF THE FOREGOING ACTIVITIES

While loving and helping your child, you will inevitably incur expenses, receive receipts, receive documents, and take photographs. These documents and things can assist you in proving your active participation in your child's life.

> # BEFORE YOU MAKE A DECISION REGARDING CUSTODY, "SOUL SEARCH" AND DO A PERSONAL INVENTORY AND ACCESSMENT OF WHY YOU WANT CUSTODY

By answering the above questions you will be able to come to grips with your actual involvement in your child's life. If you score yourself high on your personal involvement with your child, then you should move to the next inquiry as to why you want the primary physical custody of your child.

If you scored yourself low or less involved in the day-to-day activities of your child's life, be honest with yourself and evaluate what is in the best interest of your child.

Regardless of how you scored yourself or your spouse as a parent, please re-visit your shortcomings and evaluate how you can become more involved as a parent. This constructive criticism and the acting upon it should compel you to be a better parent and significantly improve your chances of becoming the primary custodial parent of your child.

WRITE A DETAILED LETTER TO YOUR ATTORNEY THAT DESCRIBES ATTRIBUTES AND SHORTCOMINGS OF BOTH PARENTS

By writing a detailed letter to your attorney that describes the attributes and shortcomings of both parents, you will be able to force yourself to soul search and assist your attorney in preparing the custody case and resolving the matter in the best interest of the children. Be sure to write on the top of each sheet and on each side of the letter that the letter is addressed to your attorney and is a

"CONFIDENTIAL ATTORNEY-CLEINT COMMUNICATION AND WORK PRODUCT."

By so describing the letter, you may prevent your spouse from using the letter against you if he or she gets his or her hands on the correspondence. Once completed, give the letter to your attorney.

BECOME MORE INVOLVED IN YOUR CHILD'S LIFE, KNOW THE PEOPLE IN YOUR CHILD'S LIFE, AND CREATE MORE FAVORABLE WITNESSES

PEOPLE WHO HAVE CONTACT WITH YOUR CHILDREN:

- ✓ Teacher:
- ✓ Day-care providers:
- ✓ Coach:
- ✓ Doctor:
- ✓ Dentist:
- ✓ Priest/pastor/rabbi/spiritual leader:
- ✓ Neighbors:
- ✓ Child's best friends:
- ✓ Boy scout/cub scout/girl scout/brownie leaders:
- ✓ School principal:
- ✓ PTA members:
- ✓ Baby sitters:
- ✓ Sunday school teacher:
- ✓ Guidance counselor:
- ✓ Relatives actively involved in child's life:
- ✓ Police officer summoned to any domestic dispute:
- ✓ Nanny:
- ✓ Housekeeper:
- ✓ Psychiatrist/sociologist/social worker:
- ✓ School nurse:
- ✓ Instructor of extracurricular activity:
- ✓ Other persons actively involved in child's life:

CORRECT YOUR BAD HABITS

We all have bad habits. Realize and work on them.

GO TO CO-PARENTING CLASSES

A child is often the victim and pawn in a couple's emotionally charged turmoil. Co-parenting courses are designed to bring parents back to the core of their responsibility to love, communicate, and take care of their child. Another goal of co-parenting classes is to emphasize the importance that although a couple no longer will be husband and wife, they will remain parents of that child. Creating a level of harmony is important for the sake of the child. Go to a co-parenting course. Every parent can be enriched by the experience.

LA-R.S. 9:306 Seminar for divorcing parents

A. Upon an affirmative showing that the facts and circumstances of the particular case before the court warrant such an order, a court exercising jurisdiction over family matters may require the parties in a custody or visitation proceeding to attend and complete a court-approved seminar designed to educate and inform the parties of the needs of the children.

B. If the court chooses to require participation in such a seminar, it shall adopt rules to accomplish the goals of Subsection A of this Section, which rules shall include but not be limited to the following:

(1) Criteria for evaluating a seminar provider and its instructors.

(2) Criteria to assure selected programs provide and incorporate into the provider's fee structure the cost of services to indigents.

(3) The amount of time a participant must take part in the program, which shall be a minimum of three hours but not exceed four hours nor shall the costs exceed twenty-five dollars per person.

(4) The time within which a party must complete the program.

C. For purposes of this Section, "instructor" means

any psychiatrist, psychologist, professional counselor, social worker licensed under state law, or in any parish other than Orleans, means a person working with a court- approved, nonprofit program of an accredited university created for educating divorcing parents with children. All instructors must have received advanced training in instructing co-parenting or similar seminars.

D. The seminar shall focus on the developmental needs of children, with emphasis on fostering the child's emotional health. The seminar shall be informative and supportive and shall direct people desiring additional information or help to appropriate resources. The course content shall contain but not be limited to the following subjects:

(1) The developmental stages of childhood, the needs of children at different ages, and age appropriate expectations of children.

(2) Stress indicators in children adjusting to divorce, the grief process, and avoiding delinquency.

(3) The possible enduring emotional effects of divorce on the child.

(4) Changing parental and marital roles.

(5) Recommendations with respect to visitation designed to enhance the child's relationship with

both parents.

(6) Financial obligations of child rearing.

(7) Conflict management and dispute resolution.

E. Nonviolent acts or communications made during the seminar, which are otherwise relevant to the subject matter of a divorce, custody, or visitation proceeding, are confidential, not subject to disclosure, and may not be used as evidence in favor of or against a participant in the pending proceeding. This rule does not require the exclusion of any evidence otherwise discoverable merely because it is presented or otherwise made during the seminar.

SINCERELY ACT IN THE "BEST INTEREST" OF YOUR CHILDREN

If you are truly a good parent, you are going to want what is best for your children. The "Best Interest" test is the pivotal legal standard used in custody disputes. The court will inquire into the quality of your relationship with your children, as well as the emotional, spiritual, educational, and health needs of each child. The court also will weigh the positive and negative attributes of each parent.

The most impressive characteristic of a parent that transcends all other aspects of custody determinations is whether a parent is sincerely acting in the best interest of his or her child.

GETTING TEMPORARY CUSTODY

As previously stated, your immediate and continued physical possession and custody of your children will significantly increase your chances of getting permanent custody. If at all possible, do the following:

1.   Keep the kids!
2.   Stay in your house with your children.
3.   Get a court order of temporary custody, pending the custody trial.

This is often a race to the courthouse so — Do it now!

IF YOU POSSESS THE CHILDREN — CONTINUE THE TRIAL DATE; IF YOU DON'T — PRESS FOR A QUICK TRIAL DATE

If you have an order of temporary custody of your children, it is to your advantage to prolong the date of the custody trial which determines the permanent custody arrangements. Judges do not like to disturb the status quo of the children's existence. The continuity of the children's living environment is an important factor in the ultimate custody determination. Remember that when the children are accustomed to the neighborhood of friends, certain schools, and churches, a judge will be hesitant to usurp then from the familiar living arrangements. Hence, ask your attorney to file for a continuance of the custody trial date.

If you are on the other side of the temporary custody fence, where you do not have the physical custody of the children, ask your attorney to expedite a trial date. Have the attorney emphasize to the judge that any undue delays in trying the custody issues shall be unfairly prejudicial to your case.

The bottom line is that temporary custody often leads to permanent custody!

KNOW WHEN AND WHAT TO TELL YOUR CHILDREN

It is a difficult thing to tell your children that you are divorcing. No matter how hard it is to do, it must be done. Once the decision has been made to divorce, the children should be told. If possible, both parents should talk with the children together. The meeting with the children should be an honest discussion of your separation. Emphasize that the break up is not their fault and that the decision to divorce is made and that they cannot change it. Do not degrade or cast blame or fault on the other parent. Frequently reassure the children that both of you are still their parents and that they are loved and will not be abandoned. Tell them that you will take care of them and keep them safe.

After you have comforted and reassured your children, inform them, as well as you can, of the proposed living arrangements, such as where each parent and child shall reside.

If one parent is absent and/or not willing to cooperate in a joint meeting with the children, speak to your children with the same honest love and affection. Continually remember to "divorce yourself from your emotions" and not degrade or blame the other parent in the presence of the children.

Anticipate that regardless of how well your discussions with your children have gone, they will likely experience some feelings of abandonment, fear, guilt, and despair. It is natural. Perhaps the best advice is to continue to communicate with your children. Tell and show them that they are loved. To some degree, they too are going through stress of the divorce process, as well.

DO NOT UNDERESTIMATE THE MATERNAL PREFERENCE

In the seventies, gender based presumptions in the law were declared unconstitutional by the United States Supreme Court. <u>Orr v. Orr</u>, 440 U.S. 268 (U.S. Supreme Court, 1979). Prior to this decision, "the tender years doctrine," which provided that the mother should have custody of infants and toddlers in their "tender years," was routinely cited as the basis of custody decisions. Mothers had to be found "unfit" to lose custody of their very young children.

Judges throughout the nation are slowly coming into the twenty-first century. Unfortunately, gender bias still exits. For generations, young children, regardless of their age, were thought to be best served by being with their mother. Various psychological and sociological studies have varied results on what is in the "best interest" of children based on their gender and age. Many courts provide preferences towards fathers for male children in their teens. As the maternal/paternal debate races on, children are being placed with a certain parent, with significant consideration given to the gender of the parent. The best way to overcome gender bias hurdles is to show the court your overwhelming involvement in your child's life.

MEDIATION

Many courts require mediation in a custody dispute.

LA-R.S. 9:332 Custody or visitation proceeding; mediation

A. The court may order the parties to mediate their differences in a custody or visitation proceeding. The mediator may be agreed upon by the parties or, upon their failure to agree, selected by the court. The court may stay any further determination of custody or visitation for a period not to exceed thirty days from the date of issuance of such an order. The court may order the costs of mediation to be paid in advance by either party or both parties jointly. The court may apportion the costs of the mediation between the parties if agreement is reached on custody or visitation. If mediation concludes without agreement between the parties, the costs of mediation shall be taxed as costs of court. The costs of mediation shall be subject to approval by the court.

B. If an agreement is reached by the parties, the mediator shall prepare a written, signed, and dated agreement. A consent judgment incorporating the agreement shall be submitted to the court for its approval.

C. Evidence of conduct or statements made in mediation is not admissible in any proceeding. This rule does not require the exclusion of any evidence otherwise discoverable merely because it is presented in the course of mediation. Facts disclosed, other than conduct or statements made in mediation, are not inadmissible by virtue of first having been disclosed in mediation.

LA-R.S. 9:333 Duties of mediator

A. The mediator shall assist the parties in formulating a written, signed, and dated agreement to mediate which shall identify the controversies between the parties, affirm the parties' intent to resolve these controversies through mediation, and specify the circumstances under which the mediation may terminate.

B. The mediator shall advise each of the parties participating in the mediation to obtain review by an attorney of any agreement reached as a result of the mediation prior to signing such an agreement.

C. The mediator shall be impartial and has no power to impose a solution on the parties.

LA-R.S. 9:334 Mediator qualifications

A. In order to serve as a qualified mediator under the provisions of this Subpart, a person shall:

(1)(a) Possess a college degree and complete a minimum of forty hours of general mediation training and twenty hours of specialized training in the mediation of child custody disputes; or

(b) Hold a license or certification as an attorney, psychiatrist, psychologist, social worker, marriage and family counselor, professional counselor, or clergyman and complete a minimum of sixteen hours of general mediation training and twenty hours of specialized training in the mediation of child custody disputes.

(2) Complete a minimum of eight hours of co-mediation training under the direct supervision of a mediator who is qualified in accordance with the provisions of Paragraph (3) of this Subsection, and who has served a minimum of fifty hours as a dispute mediator.

(3) Mediators who prior to August 15, 1997, satisfied the provisions of Paragraph (1) of this Subsection and served a minimum of fifty hours as a child custody dispute mediator are not required to complete eight hours of co- mediation training in order to serve as a qualified mediator and are qualified to supervise co-mediation training as provided in Paragraph (2) of this Subsection.

(4) Have served as a Louisiana district, appellate, or supreme court judge for at least ten years, have completed at least twenty hours of specialized mediation training in child custody disputes, and no longer be serving as a judge.

B. The training specified in Paragraph A(1) above shall include instruction as to the following:

(1) The Louisiana judicial system and judicial procedure in domestic cases.

(2) Ethical standards, including confidentiality and conflict of interests.

(3) Child development, including the impact of divorce on development.

(4) Family systems theory.

(5) Communication skills.

(6) The mediation process and required document execution.

C. A dispute mediator initially qualified under the provisions of this Subpart shall, in order to remain qualified, complete a minimum of twenty hours of clinical education in dispute mediation every two calendar years.

D. Upon request of the court, a mediator shall furnish satisfactory evidence of the following:

(1) Educational degrees, licenses and certifications.

(2) Compliance with qualifications established by this Subpart.

(3) Completion of clinical education.

E. The Louisiana State Bar Association, Alternative Dispute Resolution Section, may promulgate rules and regulations governing dispute mediator registration and qualifications, and may establish a fee not to exceed one hundred dollars for registration

CUSTODY/VISITATION EVALUATIONS — GET EXPERTS AND USE TESTS

Make sure that the evaluator interviews the children, the parents and any other person that can shed light on your attributes as a parent, your spouses' deficits as a parent, or your child's needs. The failure to request that the evaluator interview third parties is often a tragic flaw that can effect the evaluator's custody recommendation. LA-R.S. 9:331 Custody or visitation proceeding; evaluation by mental health professional

A. The court may order an evaluation of a party or the child in a custody or visitation proceeding for good cause shown. The evaluation shall be made by a mental health professional selected by the parties or by the court. The court may render judgment for costs of the evaluation, or any part thereof, against any party or parties, as it may consider equitable.

B. The court may order a party or the child to submit to and cooperate in the evaluation, testing, or interview by the mental health professional. The mental health professional shall provide the court and the parties with a written report. The mental health professional shall serve as the witness of the court, subject to cross-examination by a party.

LA-R.S. 9:331.1 Drug testing in custody or visitation proceeding

The court for good cause shown may, after a contradictory hearing, order a party in a custody or visitation proceeding to submit to specified drug tests and the collection of hair, urine, tissue, and blood samples as required by appropriate testing procedures within a time period set by the court. The refusal to submit to the tests may be taken into consideration by the court. The provisions of R.S. 9:397.2 and 397.3(A), (B), and (C) shall govern the admissibility of the test results. The fact that the court orders a drug test and the results of such test shall be confidential and shall not be admissible in any other proceedings. The court may render judgment for costs of the drug tests against any party or parties, as it may consider equitable, sufficient to cover associated costs.

PREPARE FOR A POTENTIAL VISIT FROM THE DEPARTMENT OF SOCIAL SERVICES OR A COURT APPOINTED EVALUATOR

In many custody disputes where a private sector evaluator is not used, the Department of Social Services, also referred in many states as "Family Services," provide a social worker that conducts interviews of the parents, the children, and other relevant parties. The social worker also may visit your house to inspect your living environment. Make sure that your house is clean and tidy. Traces that you are a member of the local cult or paramilitary group should be removed.

WATCH OUT FOR UNDUE INFLUENCES IN THE EVALUATION PROCESS

Some attorneys and/or parents attempt to unfairly influence the evaluation process by attempting to select or recommend an evaluator who may be prone to side with a particular gender or a particular attorney. Ask your attorney to inquire into the past personal and professional relationships between the opposing attorney and the evaluator.

Another grave concern in the evaluation process is the tendency of many parents to lie about the other parent in an attempt to gain favor with the evaluator. If you believe that your spouse might stoop to such despicable tactics, anticipate any potential lies and provide the evaluator with evidence, including other witnesses that would impeach your spouse's false statements. If your spouse is caught in a lie, you can gain significant advantage over the liar.

FIND OUT THE TRACK RECORD OF THE EVALUATOR

If you reasonably believe that the evaluator is unfairly biased towards the other side, ask your lawyer to request that the evaluator send copies of all correspondences to or from any attorney or party in your case.

CONSIDER GETTING AN INDEPENDENT EXPERT/EVALUATOR

If you reasonably believe that the evaluator's bias is overwhelming, ask your attorney to seek appointment of another evaluator. If the court refuses to change the court appointed evaluator, your attorney can request that another evaluation be conducted by a privately retained expert. This may be very expensive; however, in a hotly contested custody battle, your own expert evaluator could make all the difference.

IF THE ODDS ARE STACKED AGAINST YOU, ASK THAT VARIOUS TESTS BE CONDUCTED

Many psychological tools are now available to custody evaluators. These tests are used to evaluate whether a parent has any significant psychological disorders or personality flaws that would substantially interfere with parenting.

The MMPIT (Minnesota Multiphase Personality Inventory Test) is widely used to diagnose objectively various personality traits and abnormalities of parents and children that assist an evaluator in a custody evaluation. Without going into the details of each test, it is important to know that most psychological tests involve the evaluator's administration of the test and his or her subjective scoring and interpretation.

Tests on the children also can be used to see whether the child has any emotional, behavioral, or learning disorders that need to be addressed. Psychiatrists, sociologists and social workers conduct various tests that are used to evaluate behavior patterns and characteristics of children.

BOTH PARENTS ARE ENTITLED TO RECIEVE MEDICAL AND SCHOOL RECORDS

Pursuant to the U.S. Family Educational Rights and Privacy Act, either parent, whether custodial or noncustodial, is entitled to full access of his child's school records. Upon request, noncustodial parents are allowed to receive written documents normally sent to the custodial parent such as grades/report cards and notices of parent-teacher conferences.

Additionally, insist on notification if any health or medical conditions arise concerning your children.

LA-R.S. 9:351 Access to records of child

Notwithstanding any provision of law to the contrary, access to records and information pertaining to a minor child, including but not limited to medical, dental, and school records, shall not be denied to a parent solely because he is not the child's custodial or domiciliary parent.

> **HAVE PROVISION IN COURT ORDER/CUSTODY PLAN THAT YOUR CHILD SHALL NOT BE PLACED IN ANY SCHOOL OR CAMP WITHOUT A COURT ORDER OR WITHOUT YOUR WRITTEN PERMISSION**

> **IF THE OTHER PARENT HAS A DRUG OR ALCOHOL PROBLEM, ASK THE COURT TO CONDUCT RANDOM DRUG TESTS AND/OR ORDERS THAT THE ADDICTED PARENT GO TO ALCOHOLICS ANONYMOUS OR NARCOTICS ANONYMOUS**

It is beneficial to all concerned for a parent to seek assistance with their drug or alcohol problems. It is also important that the judge address the problem because of the potentially devastating results that could occur if the substance abuse is left unattended.

Additionally, bringing to the court's attention the legitimate substance abuse problems of the other parent, gives you a competitive advantage in the custody dispute.

Ask your attorney to seek injunctions prohibiting your spouse from drinking, being intoxicated, and/or using drugs in the presence of the children.

IN CASES OF SUBSTANCE ABUSE, INSIST ON SUPERVISED VISITATION

When your spouse has a substance abuse problem, the health and welfare of your children are in jeopardy. Your attorney should request the court to restrict the other parent's visitation privileges to supervised visitation, if not to terminate visitation.

The person supervising the visitation should be trustworthy and reliable. Courts frequently order supervised visitation and believe that the children are being adequately protected. Too often, the person ordered to supervise the visitation is irresponsible and/or is not even present at the time of the visitation sessions. Insist on a responsible party to conduct the supervision of the visitation.

RESTRICTIONS ON VISITATION

LA-R.S. 9:341 Restriction on visitation
A. Whenever the court finds by a preponderance of the evidence that a parent has subjected his or her child to physical abuse, or sexual abuse or exploitation, or has permitted such abuse or exploitation of the child, the court shall prohibit visitation between the abusive parent and the abused child until such parent proves that visitation would not cause physical, emotional, or psychological damage to the child. Should visitation be allowed, the court shall order such restrictions, conditions, and safeguards necessary to minimize any risk of harm to the child. All costs incurred in compliance with the provisions of this Section shall be borne by the abusive parent.

B. When visitation has been prohibited by the court pursuant to Subsection A, and the court subsequently authorizes restricted visitation, the parent whose visitation has been restricted shall not remove the child from the jurisdiction of the court except for good cause shown and with the prior approval of the court.

LA-R.S. 9:342 Bond to secure child custody or visitation order

For good cause shown, a court may, on its own motion or upon the motion of any party, require the posting of a bond or other security by a party to insure compliance with a child visitation order and to indemnify the other party for the payment of any costs incurred.

RETURN OF CHILD KEPT IN VIOLATION OF CUSTODY AND VISITATION ORDER

LA-R.S. 9:343 Return of child kept in violation of custody and visitation order

A. Upon presentation of a certified copy of a custody and visitation rights order rendered by a court of this state, together with the sworn affidavit of the custodial parent, the judge, who shall have jurisdiction for the limited purpose of effectuating the remedy provided by this Section by virtue of either the presence of the child or litigation pending before the court, may issue a civil warrant directed to law enforcement authorities to return the child to the custodial parent pending further order of the court having jurisdiction over the matter.

B. The sworn affidavit of the custodial parent shall include all of the following:

(1) A statement that the custody and visitation rights order is true and correct.

(2) A summary of the status of any pending custody proceeding.

(3) The fact of the removal of or failure to return the child in violation of the custody and visitation rights order.

(4) A declaration that the custodial parent desires the child returned.

VISITATION RIGHTS FOR GRANDPARENTS AND SIBLINGS

Custody is seldom awarded to grandparents when one or more of the parents are alive. Most states will allow grandparents the opportunity to file for custody or visitation. In the evaluation process of the grandparent custody/visitation requests, the courts will turn to the "best interest of the child" standard, as well as look at the general preference to award custody to the parents.

The basic ways that grandparents get legal custody of children are as follows:
1.   One or both parents have died
2.   One or both parents are incarcerated
3.   One or both parents have a substance abuse problem and/or
4.   One or both parents have been neglectful and/or abusive

Grandparent visitation can be quite beneficial to a child—if the grandparent does not play mind games with the child in an attempt to "brainwash" the child into taking sides with a particular parent or grandparent.

Courts will review the appropriateness of grandparent custody or visitation on a case by case basis. Most courts do recognize the importance of an extended family and the advantages of positive role models.

LA-R.S. 9:344 Visitation rights of grandparents and siblings

A. If one of the parties to a marriage dies, is interdicted, or incarcerated, and there is a minor child or children of such marriage, the parents of the deceased, interdicted, or incarcerated party without custody of such minor child or children may have reasonable visitation rights to the child or children of the marriage during their minority, if the court in its discretion finds that such visitation rights would be in the best interest of the child or children.

B. When the parents of a minor child or children live in concubinage and one of the parents dies, or is incarcerated, the parents of the deceased or incarcerated party may have reasonable visitation rights to the child or children during their minority, if the court in its discretion finds that such visitation rights would be in the best interest of the child or children.

C. If one of the parties to a marriage dies or is incarcerated, the siblings of a minor child or children of the marriage may have reasonable visitation rights to such child or children during their minority if the court in its discretion finds that such visitation rights would be in the best interest of the child or children.

D. If the parents of a minor child or children of the marriage are legally separated or living apart for a period of six months, the grandparents or siblings of the child or children may have reasonable visitation rights to the child or children during their minority, if the court in its discretion find that such visitation rights would be in the best interest of the child or children.

APPOINTMENT OF AN ATTORNEY TO REPRESENT CHILD IN CUSTODY OR VISITATION PROCEEDINGS

LA-R.S. 9:345 Appointment of attorney in child custody or visitation proceedings

A. In any child custody or visitation proceeding, the court, upon its own motion, upon motion of any parent or party, or upon motion of the child, may appoint an attorney to represent the child if, after a contradictory hearing, the court determines such appointment would be in the best interest of the child. In determining the best interest of the child, the court shall consider:

(1) Whether the child custody or visitation proceeding is exceptionally intense or protracted.

(2) Whether an attorney representing the child could provide the court with significant information not otherwise readily available or likely to be presented to the court.

(3) Whether there exists a possibility that neither parent is capable of providing an adequate and stable environment for the child.

(4) Whether the interests of the child and those of either parent, or of another party to the proceeding, conflict.

(5) Any other factor relevant in determining the best interest of the child.

B. The court shall appoint an attorney to represent

the child if, in the contradictory hearing, any party presents a prima facie case that a parent or other person caring for the child has sexually, physically, or emotionally abused the child or knew or should have known that the child was being abused.

C. The order appointing an attorney to represent the child shall serve as his enrollment as counsel of record on behalf of the child.

D. Upon appointment as attorney for the child, the attorney shall interview the child, review all relevant records, and conduct discovery as deemed necessary to ascertain facts relevant to the child's custody or visitation.

E. The appointed attorney shall have the right to make any motion and participate in the custody or visitation hearing to the same extent as authorized for either parent.

F. Any costs associated with the appointment of an attorney at law shall be apportioned among the parties as the court deems just, taking into consideration the parties' ability to pay. When the parties' ability to pay is limited, the court shall attempt to secure proper representation without compensation.

STOP THE OTHER PARENT FROM TAKING CHILDREN OUT OF THE STATE OR COUNTRY

Until a court has issued a ruling regarding temporary or permanent custody of the acknowledged children, either parent is free to take the child out of the state and/or even the country. Hence, you see the importance in rushing to the courthouse and request temporary custody and a temporary restraining order prohibiting the other parent from removing the child from the state and country, as well as from secreting the child in any manner.

When a custody and visitation plan is being created by the judge or the parties, insist that the order reads that neither parent shall be able to remove the child outside of the United States without an order of the court and/or without the written notarized authorization of both parties.

GET CHILD'S PASSPORT

If you have reason to be alarmed that the other parent might attempt to take your child to another country, ask the court to order the other parent to surrender his passport.

UNDERSTAND THE BASICS OF THE UNIFORM CHILD CUSTODY JURISDICTION ACT

The Uniform Child Custody Jurisdiction Act (UCCJA) has been adopted throughout the country. This legislation establishes jurisdiction across state lines.

Under the act, a state has jurisdiction for a custody dispute if the child lives in the state or has lived in the state for at least six months before one files a pleading regarding custody. Additionally, a state may have jurisdiction for a custody dispute if the child and one or more parents have a "significant connection" with the state.

A powerful tool of the UCCJA is that it allows "Emergency" jurisdiction for child custody if the child is physically present in the state and an emergency order is required to protect the child from abuse or neglect. The "Emergency" provision of the UCCJA can be a valuable shield to help protect a child from harm, yet it also provides an avenue to abuse the system in order to find a more favorable forum for a custody dispute in another state.

UNIFORM CHILD CUSTODY
JURISDICTION LAW

LA-R.S. 13:1700 Purposes of Part; construction of provisions

A. The general purposes of this part are to:

(1) Avoid jurisdictional competition and conflict with courts of other states in matters of child custody which have in the past resulted in the shifting of children from state to state with harmful effects on their well-being.

(2) Promote cooperation with the courts of other states to the end that a custody decree is rendered in that state which can best decide the case in the interest of the child.

(3) Assure that litigation concerning the custody of a child takes place ordinarily in the state with which the child and his family have the closest connection and where significant evidence concerning his care, protection, training, and personal relationships is most readily available, and to assure that the courts of this state decline the exercise of jurisdiction when the child and his family have a closer connection with another state.

(4) Discourage continuing controversies over child custody in the interest of greater stability of home environment and of secure family relationships for the child.

(5) Deter abductions and other unilateral removals of children undertaken to obtain custody awards.

(6) Avoid relitigation of custody decisions of other states in this state insofar as feasible.

(7) Facilitate the enforcement of custody decrees of other states.

(8) Promote and expand the exchange of information and other forms of mutual assistance between the courts of this state and those of other states concerned with the same child, and

(9) Make uniform the law of those states which enact it.

B. This Part shall be construed to promote the general purposes stated in this Section.

LA-R.S. 13:1702 Jurisdiction
A. A court of this state which is competent to decide child custody matters has jurisdiction to make a child custody determination by initial or modification decree if:

(1) This state (i) is the home state of the child at the time of commencement of the proceeding, or (ii) had been the child's home state within six months before commencement of the proceeding and the child is absent from this state because of his removal or retention by a person claiming his custody or for other reasons, and a parent or person acting as parent continues to live in this state; or

(2) It is in the best interest of the child that a court of this state assume jurisdiction because (i) the child and his parents, or the child and at least one contestant, have a significant connection with this state, and (ii) there is available in this state substantial evidence concerning the child's present or future care, protection, training, and personal relationships; or

(3) The child is physically present in this state and (i) the child has been abandoned or (ii) it is necessary in an emergency to protect the child because he has been subjected to or threatened with mistreatment or abuse or is otherwise neglected or dependent; or

(4) (i) It appears that no other state would have jurisdiction under prerequisites substantially in

accordance with Paragraphs (1), (2), or (3), or another state has declined to exercise jurisdiction on the ground that this state is the more appropriate forum to determine the custody of the child, and (ii) it is in the best interest of the child that this court assume jurisdiction.

B. Except under Paragraphs (3) and (4) of Subsection A, physical presence in this state of the child, or of the child and one of the contestants, is not alone sufficient to confer jurisdiction on a court of this state to make a child custody determination.

C. Physical presence of the child, while desirable, is not a prerequisite for jurisdiction to determine his custody.

LA-R.S. 13:1703 Notice and opportunity to be heard

Before making a decree under this Part, reasonable notice and opportunity to be heard shall be given to the contestants, any parent whose parental rights have not been previously terminated, and any person who has physical custody of the child. If any of these persons is outside this state, notice and opportunity to be heard shall be given pursuant to Section 1704.

LA-R.S. 13:1704 Notice to persons outside this state; submission to jurisdiction

A. Notice required for the exercise of jurisdiction over a person outside this state shall be given in a manner reasonably calculated to give actual notice, and may be:

(1) By personal delivery outside of this state in the manner prescribed for service of process within this state; or

(2) By registered or certified mail; or

(3)(a) If the party is a nonresident or absentee who cannot be served by the methods provided in Paragraphs (1) and (2) of this Subsection, either personally or through an agent for service of process, and who has not waived objection to jurisdiction, the court shall appoint an attorney at law to represent him.

(b) If the court appoints an attorney at law to represent the party, all proceedings against the party shall be conducted contradictorily against the attorney at law appointed by the court to represent him. The qualifications and duties of such attorney and his compensation shall be governed by the provisions of Articles 5092 through 5096 of the Code of Civil Procedure.

B. Notice under this Section shall be served, mailed and delivered, or last published at least ten days before any hearing in this state.

C. Proof of service outside this state may be made by affidavit of the individual who made the service, or in the manner prescribed by the law of this state, the order pursuant to which the service is made, or the law of the place in which the service is made. If service is made by mail, proof may be a receipt signed by the addressee or other evidence of delivery to the addressee.

D. Notice is not required if a person submits to the jurisdiction of the court.

LA-R.S. 13:1705 Simultaneous proceedings in other states

A. A court of this state shall not exercise its jurisdiction under this Act if at the time of filing the petition a proceeding concerning the custody of the child was pending in a court of another state exercising jurisdiction substantially in conformity with this Part, unless the proceeding is stayed by the court of the other state because this state is a more appropriate forum or for other reasons.

B. Before hearing the petition in a custody proceeding the court shall examine the pleadings and other information supplied by the parties under Section 1708 and shall consult the child custody registry established under Section 1715 concerning the pendency of proceedings with respect to the child in other states. If the court has reason to believe that proceedings may be pending in another state it shall direct an inquiry to the state court administrator or other appropriate official of the other state.

C. If the court is informed during the course of the proceeding that a proceeding concerning the custody of the child was pending in another state before the court assumed jurisdiction it shall stay the proceeding and communicate with the court in which the other proceeding is pending to the end that the issue may be litigated in the more appropriate forum and that information be exchanged in accordance with Sections 1718 through 1721. If a court of this state has made a custody decree before being informed of a pending proceeding in a court of another state it shall immediately inform that court of the fact. If the court is informed that a proceeding was commenced in another state after it assumed jurisdiction it shall likewise inform the other court to the end that the issues may be litigated in the more appropriate forum.

LA-R.S. 13:1706 Inconvenient forum

A. A court which has jurisdiction under this Part to make an initial or modification decree may decline to exercise its jurisdiction any time before making a decree if it finds that it is an inconvenient forum to make a custody determination under the circumstances of the case and that a court of another state is a more appropriate forum.

B. A finding of inconvenient forum may be made upon the court's own motion or upon motion of a party or a curator ad hoc or other representative of the child.

C. In determining if it is an inconvenient forum, the court shall consider if it is in the interest of the child that another state assume jurisdiction. For this purpose it may take into account the following factors, among others:

(1) If another state is or recently was the child's home state.

(2) If another state has a closer connection with the child and his family or with the child and one or more of the contestants.

(3) If substantial evidence concerning the child's present or future care, protection, training, and personal relationships is more readily available in another state.

(4) If the parties have agreed on another forum which is no less appropriate, and

(5) If the exercise of jurisdiction by a court of this state would contravene any of the purposes stated in Section 1700.

D. Before determining whether to decline or retain jurisdiction the court may communicate with a court of another state and exchange information pertinent to the assumption of jurisdiction by either court with a view to assuring that jurisdiction will be exercised by the more appropriate court and that a forum will be available to the parties.

E. If the court finds that it is an inconvenient forum and that a court of another state is a more appropriate forum, it may dismiss the proceedings, or it may stay the proceedings upon condition that a custody proceeding be promptly commenced in another named state or upon any other conditions which may be just and proper, including the condition that a moving party stipulate his consent and submission to the jurisdiction of the other forum.

F. The court may decline to exercise its jurisdiction under this Part if a custody determination is incidental to an action for divorce or another proceeding while retaining jurisdiction over the divorce or other proceeding.

G. If it appears to the court that it is clearly an inappropriate forum it may require the party who commenced the proceedings to pay, in addition to the costs of the proceedings in this state, necessary travel and other expenses, including attorneys' fees, incurred by other parties or their witnesses. Payment is to be made to the clerk of the court for remittance to the proper party.

H. Upon dismissal or stay of proceedings under this Section the court shall inform the court found to be the more appropriate forum of this fact, or if the court which would have jurisdiction in the other state is not certainly known, shall transmit the information to the court administrator or other appropriate official for forwarding to the appropriate court.

I. Any communication received from another state informing this state of a finding of inconvenient forum because a court of this state is the more appropriate forum shall be filed in the custody registry of the appropriate court. Upon assuming jurisdiction the court of this state shall inform the original court of this fact.

LA-R.S. 13:1707 Jurisdiction declined by reason of conduct

A. If the petitioner for an initial decree has wrongfully taken the child from another state or has engaged in similar reprehensible conduct the court may decline to exercise jurisdiction if this is just and proper under the circumstances.

B. Unless required in the interest of the child, the court shall not exercise its jurisdiction to modify a custody decree of another state if the petitioner, without consent of the person entitled to custody, has improperly removed the child from the physical custody of the person entitled to custody or has improperly retained the child after a visit or other temporary relinquishment of physical custody. If the petitioner has violated any other provision of a custody decree of another state the court may decline to exercise its jurisdiction if this is just and proper under the circumstances.

C. In appropriate cases a court dismissing a petition under this Section may charge the petitioner with necessary travel and other expenses, including attorneys' fees, incurred by other parties or their witnesses.

LA-R.S. 13:1712 Recognition of out-of-state custody decrees

The courts of this state shall recognize and enforce an initial or modification decree of a court of another state which had assumed jurisdiction under statutory provisions substantially in accordance with this Part or which was made under factual circumstances meeting the jurisdictional standards of the Part, so long as this decree has not been modified in accordance with jurisdictional standards substantially similar to those of this Act.

LA-R.S. 13:1713 Modification of custody decree of another state

A. If a court of another state has made a custody decree, a court of this state shall not modify that decree unless it appears to the court of this state that the court which rendered the decree does not now have jurisdiction under jurisdictional prerequisites substantially in accordance with this Part or has declined to assume jurisdiction to modify the decree and the court of this state has jurisdiction.

B. If a court of this state is authorized under Subsection A of this Section and Section 1707 to modify a custody decree of another state it shall give due consideration to the transcript of the record and other documents of all previous proceedings submitted to it in accordance with Section 1721.

BE CAREFUL IF YOUR SPOUSE'S LAWYER IS FIRED

On occasion a person will fire his lawyer and instruct him to immediately withdraw from the court record, in order to avoid being served pleadings and orders through the attorney. If you have concerns that your spouse may fire his attorney, ask your lawyer to request the sheriff to serve both the attorney and the other parent.

WHAT TO DO IF THE OTHER PARENT DENIES YOU ACCESS TO YOUR CHILDREN

The best action is to anticipate a problem before it arises so that your lawyer can address the possibility with the court. Hopefully, admonitions and restraining orders can be placed to prevent the denial of access to your children. If all else fails, the following are potential actions:

1. File a motion for visitation
2. File a motion to have other parent held in contempt of court if a prior order exists awarding you custody/visitation
3. Seek a reduction or suspension in child support until the other parent obeys the custody/visitation order
4. File a motion to modify the prior custody/visitation order
5. File a motion for sole custody

6. File a motion seeking the other party to post a bond to insure your custody/visitation rights
7. Ask your attorney for other advice and/or
8. Seek assistance from law enforcement officers to enforce a custody/visitation order

Regrettably, sometimes there are reasons to deny access, i.e., for abuse, neglect and/or substance abuse problems that affect the children. Courts, counselors, child protection agencies, battered women shelters, and law enforcement agencies are prepared to deal with these problems.

SPECIFY THE VISITATION RIGHTS

When working on a visitation plan for both parents, it is usually a great error to simply allow for "reasonable" or "liberal" visitation. A custody and visitation plan or order that merely contains this language is a plan or order that does not address the real world problems of visitation disputes. If the term "reasonable" is used in the visitation plan, the parent seeking the visitation is subject to the whims of the primary custodial parent. What is "reasonable" to one parent may be quite "unreasonable" to the other.

The best way to avoid the nightmares that can exist with a lazy visitation plan, is to insist on specified visitation. A visitation plan that explicitly identifies the dates and times of visitation will not be subject to the whims of one parent or the interpretation of either parent.

CHECKLIST TO ASSIST IN CREATING A VISITATION SCHEDULE

- ❏ Birthdays
- ❏ Christmas Eve/Day/Holiday
- ❏ Graduations
- ❏ Grandparent Events/Other Relative Special Occasions
- ❏ Easter Day/Holiday
- ❏ Extracurricular Activities
- ❏ Hanukkah
- ❏ Father's Day
- ❏ Halloween
- ❏ July 4th
- ❏ Labor Day
- ❏ Mardi Gras
- ❏ Memorial Day
- ❏ Mother's Day
- ❏ New Year's Eve/Day
- ❏ Sporting Events
- ❏ Thanksgiving Day/Holiday
- ❏ Spring Break
- ❏ Summer Vacation
- ❏ Other dates or Occasions that have special meanings

MAXIMIZE YOUR VISITATION RIGHTS

A child has the general right to continue his relationship with both parents. Parents seeking visitation should consider maximizing their specified dates of visitation. Remember to design a visitation plan that will be compatible with your work schedule.

Your imagination may be the limit to what days you may seek. Consider the following:
Any holiday recognized by your local, state or federal government
(Ask a florist—they have holidays for everything under the sun!)

FORMALLY AGREE ON COST ARRANGEMENTS INVOLVED WITH VISITATION AND TRAVEL

Often parties agree to visitation schedules without having a formal agreement as to who pays the cost of any travel involved. Have a written agreement and/or order that sets forth the financial responsibilities associated with any travel involved in the visitation process.

ALLOWING VISITATION CREATES
A FREE BABY-SITTER

Many people that are in a heated contested custody or visitation dispute often forget that allowing visitation allows for a free baby-sitter. The thirst for your spouse's blood often clouds one's view of your future needs and desires. Months down the road, you may want a break from your children to go to the beach or take a vacation with a new lover.

GET MORE VISITATION AND
PERHAPS PAY LESS CHILD SUPPORT

In most states, child support guidelines and schedules are based on the parent receiving visitation having average visitation rights such as having the children on alternating weekends, alternating major holidays and several weeks during the summer. If you receive visitation rights that are greater than the visitation rights normally given by the court, ask your lawyer to seek for a decrease in your child support obligation as you are incurring expenses in support of your children when they are in your custody that was not envisioned by the child support schedule.

IF THE OTHER PARENT DOES NOT USE HIS OR HER VISITATION RIGHTS, ASK FOR MORE CHILD SUPPORT AND/OR PAYMENT FOR BABY-SITTING

Again, if your child support guidelines envision average visitation, and the other parent is not taking the children during his scheduled visitation days, then ask your attorney to seek an increase in child support for the extra days and nights that you have custody of your children. An alternative is to ask the court to order the other parent to pay or reimburse for extra food, utilities, daycare or baby-sitting expenses incurred because he did not pick up the children pursuant to the visitation plan.

Most courts will not compel a parent to exercise his visitation rights; however, a court is much more likely to award you money for the extra expenses incurred because of your unanticipated cost of keeping the children when the other parent should have.

IF YOUR CHILD DOES NOT WANT TO SEE THE OTHER PARENT, INFORM YOUR ATTORNEY AND THE COURT

Frequently, children do not wish to have visitation with the non-custodial parent. When this occurs, immediately inform your attorney. Whether or not your child's hesitancy has any valid basis may ultimately be determined by the judge. By informing your attorney and allowing him to inform the court of the problem, then you have diminished the chances that the court would sanction you for interfering in the other parent's visitation rights. If you do not inform your attorney of the problem, then the other parent might allege that you are persuading your child to resist visitation. Let the court and/or the court's evaluator to get to the heart of the problem.

INSIST ON ADDRESSES AND TELEPHONE NUMBERS AND MAXIMIZE TELEPHONE ACCESS

The parent with the physical custody of the children may attempt to prohibit or restrict your physical or telephone access to your children. Insist that you have the addresses and telephone numbers of each place where the children shall be residing. Additionally, you may wish to have an agreement on the minimum and maximum telephone calls the noncustodial parent can have with the children. A court order delineating the agreement shall assist in eliminating future problems.

If the parents are cooperative, reasonable open access to the children is preferable.

KNOW WHEN TO REQUEST A MODIFICATION OF VISITATION RIGHTS

The custodial parent may wish to request a change in the visitation schedule if the other parent routinely refuses to honor the visitation plan and/or refuses to return the child at the designated time and place.

WATCH OUT FOR "CUSTODY BLACKMAIL"

As stated in the alimony and child support chapters of this book, be aware of any attempts on the part of your spouse to threaten a custody battle when he or she really does not want physical custody, but merely seeks financial advantage in another area of dispute. These threats of a custody battle are often used in a hidden or blatant agenda for a spouse to make monetary concessions. If this occurs, speak to your attorney about these attempts to intimidate.

RELOCATION OF CHILDREN

LA-R.S. 9:355.3 Notice of proposed relocation of child to other parent

A. A parent entitled to primary custody of a child shall notify the other parent of a proposed relocation of the child's principal residence as required by R.S. 9:355.4.

B. If both parents have equal physical custody of a child, a parent shall notify the other parent of a proposed relocation of the child's principal residence as required by R.S. 9:355.4.

C. In the absence of a court order or express written agreement confected by the parties which designates the principal residence of a child, a parent shall notify the other parent of a proposed relocation of the child's principal residence as required by R.S. 9:355.4.

LA-R.S. 9:355.4 Mailing notice of proposed relocation address A. Notice of a proposed relocation of the principal residence of a child shall be given by registered or certified mail, return receipt requested, to the last known address of the parent no later than either:

(1) The sixtieth day before the date of the intended move or proposed relocation.

(2) The tenth day after the date that the parent knows the information required to be furnished by Subsection B of this Section, if the parent did not know and could not reasonably have known the information in sufficient time to comply with the sixty-day notice, and it is not reasonably possible to extend the time for relocation of the child.

B. The following information, if available, shall be included with the notice of intended relocation of the child:

(1) The intended new residence, including the specific address, if known.

(2) The mailing address, if not the same.

(3) The home telephone number, if known.

(4) The date of the intended move or proposed relocation.

(5) A brief statement of the specific reasons for the proposed relocation of a child, if applicable.

(6) A proposal for a revised schedule of visitation with the child.

C. A parent required to give notice of a proposed relocation shall have a continuing duty to provide the information required by this Section as that information becomes known.

LA-R.S. 9:355.5 Court authorization to relocate

A parent seeking to relocate the principal residence of a child shall not, absent consent, remove the child pending resolution of dispute, or final order of the court, unless the parent obtains a temporary order to do so pursuant to R.S. 9:355.10.

LA-R.S. 9:355.6 Failure to give notice of relocation or relocation without court authorization
The court may consider a failure to provide notice of a proposed relocation of a child or relocation without court authorization as provided by R.S. 9:355.3 and 355.4 as:

(1) A factor in making its determination regarding the relocation of a child.

(2) A basis for ordering the return of the child if the relocation has taken place without notice or court authorization.

(3) Sufficient cause to order the parent seeking to relocate the child to pay reasonable expenses and attorney fees incurred by the person objecting to the relocation.

LA-R.S. 9:355.7 Failure to object to notice of proposed relocation

The primary custodian of a child or a parent who has equal physical custody may relocate the principal residence of a child after providing notice as provided by R.S. 9:355.3 and 355.4, unless the parent entitled to notice initiates a proceeding seeking a temporary or permanent order to prevent the relocation within twenty days after the receipt of the notice.

LA-R.S. 9:355.8 Objection to relocation of child

A. A parent must initiate a summary proceeding objecting to a proposed relocation of the principal residence of a child within twenty days after receipt of notice and seek a temporary or permanent order to prevent the relocation.

B. Upon request of a copy of notice of objection, the court may promptly appoint an independent mental health expert to render a determination as to whether the proposed relocation is in the best interest of the child.

LA-R.S. 9:355.9 Priority for temporary and final hearing

A hearing on either a temporary or permanent order permitting or restricting relocation shall be accorded appropriate priority on the court's docket.

LA-R.S. 9:355.10 Temporary order

A. The court may grant, after a notice of objection has been filed, a temporary order allowing a parent to relocate.

B. The court, upon the request of the moving parent, may hold a limited evidentiary hearing on the proposed relocation but may not grant court authorization to remove the child on an ex parte basis.

C. If the court issues a temporary order authorizing a parent to relocate with the child, the court may not give undue weight to the temporary relocation as a factor in reaching its final determination.

D. If temporary relocation of a child is permitted, the court may require the parent relocating the child to provide reasonable security guaranteeing that the court ordered visitation with the child will not be interrupted or interfered with by the relocating parent or that the relocating parent will return the child if court authorization for the removal is denied at the final hearing.

LA-R.S. 9:355.11 Proposed relocation not basis for modification

Providing notice of a proposed relocation of a child shall not constitute a change of circumstance warranting a change of custody. Moving without prior notice or moving in violation of a court order may constitute a change of circumstances warranting a modification of custody.

LA-R.S. 9:355.12 Factors to determine contested relocation In reaching its decision regarding a proposed relocation, the court shall consider the following factors:

(1) The nature, quality, extent of involvement, and duration of the child's relationship with the parent proposing to relocate and with the non-relocating parent, siblings, and other significant persons in the child's life.

(2) The age, developmental stage, needs of the child, and the likely impact the relocation will have on the child's physical, educational, and emotional development, taking into consideration any special needs of the child.

(3) The feasibility of preserving the relationship between the non-relocating parent and the child through suitable visitation arrangements, considering the logistics and financial circumstances of the parties.

(4) The child's preference, taking into consideration the age and maturity of the child.

(5) Whether there is an established pattern of conduct of the parent seeking the relocation, either to promote or thwart the relationship of the child and the non-relocating party.

(6) Whether the relocation of the child will enhance

the general quality of life for both the custodial parent seeking the relocation and the child, including but not limited to financial or emotional benefit or educational opportunity.

(7) The reasons of each parent for seeking or opposing the relocation.

(8) Any other factors affecting the best interest of the child.

LA-R.S. 9:355.13 Burden of proof

The relocating parent has the burden of proof that the proposed relocation is made in good faith and is in the best interest of the child.

LA-R.S. 9:355.14 Posting security

If relocation of a child is permitted, the court may require the parent relocating the child to provide reasonable security guaranteeing that the court ordered visitation with the child will not be interrupted or interfered with by the relocating party.

LA-R.S. 9:355.15 Application of factors at initial hearing
If the issue of relocation is presented at the initial hearing to determine custody of and visitation with a child, the court shall apply the factors set forth in R.S. 9:355.12 in making its initial determination.

LA-R.S. 9:355.16 Sanctions for unwarranted or frivolous proposal to relocate child or objection to relocation

A. After notice and a reasonable opportunity to respond, the court may impose a sanction on a parent proposing a relocation of the child or objecting to a proposed relocation of a child if it determines that the proposal was made or the objection was filed:

(1) To harass the other parent or to cause unnecessary delay or needless increase in the cost of litigation.

(2) Without being warranted by existing law or based on a frivolous argument.

(3) Based on allegations and other factual contentions which have no evidentiary support nor, if specifically so identified, could not have been reasonably believed to be likely to have evidentiary support after further investigation.

B. A sanction imposed under this Section shall be limited to what is sufficient to deter repetition of such conduct or comparable conduct by others similarly situated. The sanction may consist of, or include, directives of a nonmonetary nature, an order to pay a penalty to the court, or, if imposed on motion and warranted for effective deterrence, an order directing payment to the movant of some or all of the reasonable attorney fees and other expenses incurred as a direct result of the violation.

LA-R.S. 9:355.17 Continuing jurisdiction

If the court grants authorization to relocate, the court may retain continuing, exclusive jurisdiction of the case after relocation of the child as long as the non-relocating parent remains in the state.

CHAPTER 5

CHILD SUPPORT

The purpose of a child support award is to provide financial assistance for a child based on the average monthly expenses associated with that child. The child support award should be based on the proportionate income or earnings capacity of the parents.

Each state has implemented child support guidelines to assist the courts with a means of calculating what is legislatively presumed to be sufficient for the child's needs and which is fair relative to the parents' earnings. Only 6.2 million (approximately half) of the 11.5 million custodial parents have a child support award or agreement. Mothers receive child support awards at a higher rate than fathers. Annually, over 5 million custodial parents live without any award of child support from the other parent. Reasons for not seeking a child support award include that the custodial parent does not want child support and that the other parent can not afford to pay child support. Approximately one-third of the 5 million parents without child support awards decided not to seek child support. 1996 statistics show that a mere sixty-seven (67%) percent (or $11.9 billion dollars) of the $17.7 billion dollars of child support due to custodial parents is paid. (U.S. Census Bureau).

Only half of custodial parents that have an order or agreement for child support receive payment in full. Unfortunately, approximately 25 percent of all custodial parents receive only partial payment. Worst of all, another 25 percent of custodial parents don't receive any child support at all.

Approximately, 90 percent of fathers who have joint custody pay child support, while 80 percent of fathers who receive visitation pay child support. (The U. S. Census Bureau; American Bar Association).

State prosecutors report that approximately 2 to 5 percent of their child support cases involve mothers who owe past due child support. (American Bar Association).

Before a child support order can be made, paternity/maternity must be established. Paternity is discussed in a prior chapter.

STANDARD OF LIVING

Mothers who receive child support have a lower annual income (Average $18,144 per year) versus their male counterparts receiving child support who have an average income of $33,579 per year. Less than 5 percent of divorced or separated women raising children of the marriage receive alimony. Approximately 42 percent receive child support, and the average amount received by them is approximately $125 per child per month. (U.S. Census Bureau)

A widely cited study discovered that a year after a divorce, the standard of living of women and children drops by an average 73 percent, while men's standard of living actually increases an average of 42 percent. (Lenore Weitzman, "The Economics of Divorce: Social and Economic Consequences of Property, Alimony, and Child Support Awards," UCLA Law Review 28:1181, 1245 (1981).) Approximately one-third of all female headed families with children live in poverty.

LA-Art. 141. Child support; authority of court

In a proceeding for divorce or thereafter, the court may order either or both of the parents to provide an interim allowance or final support for a child based on the needs of the child and the ability of the parents to provide support.

The court may award an interim allowance only when a demand for final support is pending.

LA-C.C. Art. 142 Modification or termination of child support award

An award of child support may be modified if the circumstances of the child or of either parent materially change and shall be terminated upon proof that it has become unnecessary.

LA-C.C. Art. 227 Parental support and education of children

Fathers and mothers, by the very act of marrying, contract together the obligation of supporting, maintaining, and educating their children.

LA-C.C. Art. 3501.1 Actions for arrearages of child support

An action to make executory arrearages of child support is subject to a liberative prescription of ten years.

CHILD SUPPORT MODELS

There are two basic models for child support:
1. Fixed child support payments that have no provisions for future modifications
2. Escalator Clause/Variable child support payments that periodically change proportionate to actual changes in the parents' income, the consumer price index (CPI), or some other variable

CHILD SUPPORT GUIDELINES

Federal law requires each state to create child support guidelines. (42 U.S.C. 667) Child support guidelines presume that parents with similar incomes should be required to pay relatively equal amounts in child support. Likewise, a further goal of the implementation of child support guidelines is to prevent large variability in the child support awards under similar circumstances. Unfortunately, our national and state systems are seriously flawed as they operate under a false premise that people can accurately calculate child support figures and that parents will not misrepresent their income and/or earnings capacity. A significant danger for you lies in a haphazard implementation of your state's child support guidelines as your child may suffer financially from the miscalculations and/or misrepresentations. The only key to safeguard you and your child from such neglect and abuse is to know the pitfalls and to benefit from the knowledge that you will gain from the following information.

GUIDELINES FOR DETERMINATION OF CHILD SUPPORT OBLIGATION

LA-R.S. 9:315 Economic data and principles; definitions

A. Basic principles. The premise of these guidelines as well as the provisions of the Civil Code is that child support is a continuous obligation of both parents, children are entitled to share in the current income of both parents, and children should not be the economic victims of divorce or out-of- wedlock birth. The economic data underlying these guidelines, which adopt the Income Shares Model, and the guideline calculations attempt to simulate the percentage of parental net income that is spent on children in intact families incorporating a consideration of the expenses of the parties, such as federal and state taxes and FICA taxes. While the legislature acknowledges that the expenditures of two-household divorced, separated, or non-formed families are different from intact family households, it is very important that the children of this state not be forced to live in poverty because of family disruption and that they be afforded the same opportunities available to children in intact families, consisting of parents with similar financial means to those of their own parents.

B. Economic data.

(1) The Incomes Shares approach to child support guidelines incorporates a numerical schedule of support amounts. The schedule provides economic estimates of child-rearing expenditures for various income levels and numbers of children in the household. The schedule is composed of economic data utilizing a table of national averages adjusted to reflect Louisiana's status as a low-income state and to incorporate a self-sufficiency reserve for low-

income obligors to form the basic child support obligation.

(2) In intact families, the income of both parents is pooled and spent for the benefit of all household members, including the children. Each parent's contribution to the combined income of the family represents his relative sharing of household expenses. This same income sharing principle is used to determine how the parents will share a child support award.

C. Definitions. As used in this Part:

(1) "Adjusted gross income" means gross income, minus amounts for preexisting child support or spousal support obligations paid to another who is not a party to the proceedings, or on behalf of a child who is not the subject of the action of the court.

(2) "Combined adjusted gross income" means the combined adjusted gross income of both parties.

(3) "Extraordinary medical expenses" means uninsured expenses over one hundred dollars for a single illness or condition. It includes but is not limited to reasonable and necessary costs for orthodontia, dental treatment, asthma treatment, physical therapy, uninsured chronic health problems, and professional counseling or psychiatric therapy for diagnosed mental disorders.

(4) "Gross income" means:

(a) The income from any source, including but not limited to salaries, wages, commissions, bonuses, dividends, severance pay, pensions, interest, trust income, annuities, capital gains, social security benefits, workers' compensation benefits, unemployment insurance benefits, disability insurance benefits, and spousal support received from a preexisting spousal support obligation;

(b) Expense reimbursement or in-kind payments received by a parent in the course of employment, self-employment, or operation of a business, if the reimbursements or payments are significant and reduce the parent's personal living expenses. Such payments include but are not limited to a company car, free housing, or reimbursed meals; and

(c) Gross receipts minus ordinary and necessary expenses required to produce income, for purposes of income from self-employment, rent, royalties, proprietorship of a business, or joint ownership or a partnership or closely held corporation. "Ordinary and necessary expenses" shall not include amounts allowable by the Internal Revenue Service for the accelerated component of depreciation expenses or investment tax credits or any other business expenses determined by the court to be inappropriate for determining gross income for purposes of calculating child support.

(d) As used herein, "gross income" does not include:

(i) Child support received, or benefits received from public assistance programs, including Family Independence Temporary Assistance Plan, supplemental security income, food stamps, and general assistance.

(ii) Per diem allowances which are not subject to federal income taxation under the provisions of the Internal Revenue Code.

(iii) Extraordinary overtime including but not limited to income attributed to seasonal work regardless of its percentage of gross income when, in the court's discretion, the inclusion thereof would be inequitable to a party.

(5) "Health insurance premiums" means the actual amount paid by a party for providing health insurance on behalf of the child. It does not include any amount paid by an employer or any amounts paid for coverage of any other persons. If more than one dependent is covered by health insurance which is paid through a lump-sum dependent-coverage premium, and not all of such dependents are the subject of the guidelines calculation, the cost of the coverage shall be prorated among the dependents covered before being applied to the guidelines.

(6) "Income" means:

(a) Actual gross income of a party, if the party is employed to full capacity; or

(b) Potential income of a party, if the party is voluntarily unemployed or underemployed. A party shall not be deemed voluntarily unemployed or underemployed if he or she is absolutely unemployable or incapable of being employed, or if the unemployment or underemployment results through no fault or neglect of the party.

(c) The court may also consider as income the benefits a party derives from expense-sharing or other sources; however, in determining the benefits of expense-sharing, the court shall not consider the income of another spouse, regardless of the legal regime under which the remarriage exists, except to the extent that such income is used directly to reduce the cost of a party's actual expenses.

(7) "Net child care costs" means the reasonable costs of child care incurred by a party due to employment or job search, minus the value of the federal income tax credit for child care.

REBUTTABLE PRESUMPTION

Louisiana law creates a "legal fiction" as it presumes that the guidelines represent the child support financial requirements of an average Louisiana parent. The presumption that the guidelines are appropriate for your children's' support is rebuttable whereby allowing a deviation from the guidelines in cases where there is proof of special financial needs not anticipated in the guideline formulation.

LA-R.S. 9:315.1 Rebut table presumption; deviation from guidelines by court; stipulations by parties

A. The guidelines set forth in this Part are to be used in any proceeding to establish or modify child support filed on or after October 1, 1989. There shall be a rebut table presumption that the amount of child support obtained by use of the guidelines set forth in this Part is the proper amount of child support.

B. The court may deviate from the guidelines set forth in this Part if their application would not be in the best interest of the child or would be inequitable to the parties. The court shall give specific oral or written reasons for the deviation, including a finding as to the amount of support that would have been required under a mechanical application of the guidelines and the particular facts and circumstances that warranted a deviation from the guidelines. The reasons shall be made part of the record of the proceedings.

C. In determining whether to deviate from the guidelines, the court's considerations may include:

(1) That the combined adjusted gross income of the parties is not within the amounts shown on the schedule in R.S. 9:315.19.

(a) If the combined adjusted gross income of the parties is less than the lowest sum shown on the schedule, the court shall determine an amount of child support based on the facts of the case, except that the amount awarded shall not be less than the minimum child support provided in R.S. 9:315.14.

(b) If the combined adjusted gross income of the parties exceeds the highest sum shown on the schedule, the court shall determine an amount of child support as provided in R.S. 9:315.13(B).

(2) The legal obligation of a party to support dependents who are not the subject of the action before the court and who are in that party's household.

(3) That in a case involving one or more families, consisting of children none of whom live in the household of the noncustodial or nondomiciliary parent but who have existing child support orders (multiple families), the court may use its discretion in setting the amount of the basic child support obligation, provided it is not below the minimum fixed by R.S. 9:315.14, if the existing child support orders reduce the noncustodial or nondomiciliary parent's income below the lowest income level on the schedule contained in R.S. 9:315.19.

(4) The extraordinary medical expenses of a party, or extraordinary medical expenses for which a party may be responsible, not otherwise taken into consideration under the guidelines.

(5) An extraordinary community debt of the parties.

(6) The need for immediate and temporary support for a child when a full hearing on the issue of support is pending but cannot be timely held. In such cases, the court at the full hearing shall use the provisions of this Part and may redetermine support without the necessity of a change of circumstances being shown.

(7) The permanent or temporary total disability of a spouse to the extent such disability diminishes his present and future earning capacity, his need to save adequately for uninsurable future medical costs, and other additional costs associated with such disability, such as transportation and mobility costs, medical expenses, and higher insurance premiums.

(8) Any other consideration which would make application of the guidelines not in the best interest of the child or children or inequitable to the parties.

D. The court may review and approve a stipulation between the parties entered into after the effective date of this Part as to the amount of child support to be paid. If the court does review the stipulation, the court shall consider the guidelines set forth in this Part to review the adequacy of the stipulated amount and may require the parties to provide the court with the income statements and documentation required by R.S. 9:315.2.

CALCULATION OF BASIC CHILD SUPPORT

The first step in determining appropriate child support is to calculate the basic child support obligation as determined by using the guidelines and worksheet. Other child care expenses may be added to this figure while other deductions can be made as well.

LA-R.S. 9:315.2 Calculation of basic child support obligation

A. Each party shall provide to the court a verified income statement showing gross income and adjusted gross income, together with documentation of current and past earnings. Spouses of the parties shall also provide any relevant information with regard to the source of payments of household expenses upon request of the court or the opposing party, provided such request is filed in a reasonable time prior to the hearing. Failure to timely file the request shall not be grounds for a continuance. Suitable documentation of current earnings shall include but not be limited to pay stubs, employer statements, or receipts and expenses if self-employed. The documentation shall include a copy of the party's most recent federal tax return. A copy of the statement and documentation shall be provided to the other party.

B. If a party is voluntarily unemployed or underemployed, his or her gross income shall be determined as set forth in R.S. 9:315.11.

C. The parties shall combine the amounts of their adjusted gross incomes. Each party shall then determine by percentage his or her proportionate share of the combined amount. The amount obtained for each party is his or her percentage share of the combined adjusted gross income.

D. The court shall determine the basic child support obligation amount from the schedule in R.S. 9:315.19 by using the combined adjusted gross income of the parties and the number of children involved in the proceeding, but in no event shall the amount of child support be less than the amount provided in R.S. 9:315.14.

E. After the basic child support obligation has been established, the total child support obligation shall be determined as hereinafter provided in this Part.

ASK FOR CONTRIBUTIONS FOR "EXTRAS"

In order to insure that each parent is financially responsible for his proportionate share of all child-related expenses, instruct your attorney to seek contributions for the other parent's proportionate share of all insurance deductibles, co-payments, and payments not covered by insurance. These "Extra" expenses can quickly add up. Don't let these dollars slip through the hands that help your child.

- Medical expenses and medical insurance
- Dental expenses and dental insurance
- Extraordinary medical expenses (orthodontic/psychiatrist/counseling/miscellaneous health-related expenses)
- Day-care expenses
- Tuition/educational expenses
- Extraordinary non-medical related expenses

NET CHILD CARE COSTS

Net child care costs are an addition to the basic child support obligation as calculated pursuant to LA-R.S. 9:315.3.

LA-R.S. 9:315.3 Net child care costs; addition to basic obligation

Net child care costs shall be added to the basic child support obligation. The net child care costs are determined by applying the Federal Credit for Child and Dependent Care Expenses provided in Internal Revenue Form 2441 to the total or actual child care costs.

GET DAY-CARE

Daycare is a common and important expense that significantly can add to a parent's child support obligation. Inquire with your attorney as to whether day-care expenses are included in the basic child support award or whether you should request it as an additional child-related expense.

The actual day-care expense incurred is usually under the discretion of the primary domiciliary parent. That parent usually chooses the day-care facility and resulting costs.

ASK THE COURT FOR PARTICIPATION IN THE DECISION REGARDING WHICH DAY-CARE FACILITY IS USED

By assisting in the choice of the day-care facility, you also participate in cost control.

REPLACE DAY-CARE WITH YOUR CARE OR THAT OF RELATIVES

A parent may be able to significantly decrease the day-care expense by asking relatives to baby-sit. Grandparents and adult siblings often are more than willing to assist with this supervision. Your own physical care of your child can decrease the cost of day-care. Ask for the "right of first refusal" of having the physical possession of the child in events when the child would otherwise be at the day-care center or with a baby-sitter.

A parent may argue that having relatives provide baby-sitting services is inferior to a day-care facility as the day-care center may allow the child to gain socialization skills.

PLACE CHILD IN CHOSEN DAY-CARE FACILITY PRIOR TO COURT DATE

Judges are quite hesitant to remove a child from a day-care facility once the child has commenced attending the center. Many attorneys believe that it is prudent to register and put your child into a day-care facility prior to the child support and/or custody trial date as the parent shall be able to show stability in the child's life and provide evidence of actual day-care expenses. If a parent does not have the child in previously registered and/or attending a day-care facility, then the other parent will have greater chances to impeach the need for day-care, the choice of day-care, and the expense of day-care.

HEALTH INSURANCE PREMIUMS

Only about 40% of child support awards include medical insurance benefits as part of that award. Unfortunately, another 31% of those parents who were ordered to provide health insurance for their children failed or refused to provide it. Likewise, of the non-custodial parents who were not ordered to provide health insurance, 18% provided such insurance without an order. (U.S. Census Bureau)

Medical and dental expenses associated with your child should be included in the calculation and implementation of a child support award and related child care obligations. All orthodontic, psychiatric, and related needs of your child should be brought to the attention of your attorney.

If you anticipate certain future expenses for your child that have not yet arisen, ask your attorney to seek provisions in the child support order that compel the other parent to pay for a proportionate share of these expenses as they arise. This shall prevent you from having to pay your attorney to go back into court at a later date to seek this relief.

Health care insurance premiums also are added or subtracted from the basic child care obligation depending on which parent pays for the health insurance. It is important to provide your attorney with a break down of the premium allocated to each child by the insurance provider or employer.

LA-R.S. 9:315.4 Health insurance premiums; addition to basic obligation

In any child support case, the court may order one of the parties to enroll or maintain an insurable child in a health benefits plan, policy, or program. In determining which party should be required to enroll the child or to maintain such insurance on behalf of the child, the court shall consider each party's individual, group, or employee's health insurance program, employment history, and personal income and other resources. The cost of health insurance premiums incurred on behalf of the child shall be added to the basic child support obligation.

EXTRAORDINARY MEDICAL EXPENSES

Extraordinary medial expenses are those incurred under circumstances of special medial treatment of a child. Louisiana courts consider "extraordinary medical expenses" to commence when those special medical treatments cost over $100 in a month or $1,000 in a year. Hence, it is important to request your attorney to ask the court or the opposing party for an order of support which includes an allocation of the special medical expenses under $100 per month; otherwise one parent may get stuck with paying the $89 monthly asthma medication expense without contribution from the other parent. Make your attorney acutely aware of any such special medial and/or pharmacy expenses.

LA-R.S. 9:315.5 Extraordinary medical expenses; addition to basic obligation

By agreement of the parties or order of the court, extraordinary medical expenses incurred on behalf of the child shall be added to the basic child support obligation.

OTHER EXTRAORDINARY EXPENSES

These "Extraordinary Expenses" generally include tuition, books, supplies, educational transportation expenses, and extracurricular expenses. Such expenses are largely subject to the discretion of the Court.

Like day-care, school tuition is an expense that can be quite costly. Inquire with your attorney as to your rights associated with school expenses. Your attorney should ask for the other parent's contribution toward tuition, school loan interest payments, uniforms, school books, supplies, and school extracurricular expenses.

Judges generally have the discretion to determine whether a parent should be obligated to pay the additional expense for a child to attend a private or parochial school instead of a public institution. Many judges require a parent to prove that the child has a special need which would require the child to attend the private or parochial school. Yet, judges are reluctant to remove a child who already attends the private or parochial school. The court will look to the "best interest of the child" standard. Continuity of the child's life is very important.
Quick Fact

Thirty four (34%) percent of America's three- and four-year-olds are enrolled in nursery schools. (U.S. Census Bureau)

LA-R.S. 9:315.6 Other extraordinary expenses; addition to basic obligation

By agreement of the parties or order of the court, the following expenses incurred on behalf of the child may be added to the basic child support obligation:

(1) Expenses of tuition, registration, books, and supply fees required for attending a special or private elementary or secondary school to meet the needs of the child.

(2) Any expenses for transportation of the child from one party to the other.

ENTERING INTO A CONSENT AGREEMENT AND ORDER WHEREBY THE PARENTS AGREE TO PAY FOR COLLEGE EDUCATION

Although it may not be otherwise enforceable in Louisiana, if both parents are agreeable to the general child support provisions, it may be a good time to propose an agreement regarding the payment of your child's college education. If both parents enter into such an agreement and it is converted into a judgment of the court, it may be enforceable at a later date. There does not appear to be any harm in trying to get an agreement that benefits the future of your child.

DEDUCTIONS FOR INCOME OF THE CHILD

Although deductions have been made for a child who has been working, remember that there should not be a deduction on this basis if the child has earned the income while a full-time student.

LA-R.S. 9:315.7 Deductions for income of the child

A. Income of the child that can be used to reduce the basic needs of the child may be considered as a deduction from the basic child support obligation.

B. The provisions of this Section shall not apply to income earned by a child while a full-time student, regardless of whether such income was earned during a summer or holiday break.

C. The provisions of this Section shall not apply to benefits received by a child from public assistance programs, including but not limited to Family Independence Temporary Assistance Programs (FITAP), food stamps, or any means- tested program.

CALCULATION OF TOTAL CHILD SUPPORT

<u>It is not recommended that you try to calculate your own child support figures</u>. In my many years of law practice, I have found the most of my clients who have attempted to calculate their own figures generally come up with an incorrect figure over 90% of the time. I have encountered many an attorney who does not regularly practice family law make these mistakes. Hence, I recommend that you confer with your attorney and provide him or her with the information and let them make the calculations. The calculation is too important to allow for a mistake. The Louisiana Family Law Guide provides you with the schedule and worksheets, but please be on guard that mistakes in calculation are quite common. Let your attorney do the work for you.

LA-R.S. 9:315.8 Calculation of total child support obligation; worksheet

A. The total child support obligation shall be determined by adding together the basic child support obligation amount, the net child care costs, the cost of health insurance premiums, extraordinary medical expenses, and other extraordinary expenses.

B. A deduction, if any, for income of the child shall then be subtracted from the amount calculated in Subsection A. The remaining amount is the total child support obligation.

C. Each party's share of the total child support obligation shall then be determined by multiplying his or her percentage share of combined adjusted gross income times the total child support obligation.

D. The party without legal custody or nondomiciliary party shall owe his or her total child support obligation as a money judgment of child support to the custodial or domiciliary party, minus any court-ordered direct payments made on behalf of the child for work-related net child care costs, health insurance premiums, extraordinary medical expenses, or extraordinary expenses provided as adjustments to the schedule.

E. "Joint Custody" means a joint custody order that is not shared custody as defined in R.S. 9:315.9.

(1) In cases of joint custody, the court shall consider the period of time spent by the child with the nondomiciliary party as a basis for adjustment to the amount of child support to be paid during that period of time.

(2) If under a joint custody order, the person ordered to pay child support has physical custody of the child for more than seventy-three days, the court may order a credit to the child support obligation. A day for the purposes of this Paragraph shall be determined by the court; however, in no instance shall less than four hours of physical custody of the child constitute a day.

(3) In determining the amount of credit to be given, the court shall consider the following:

(a) The amount of time the child spends with the person to whom the credit would be applied.

(b) The increase in financial burden placed on the person to whom the credit would be applied and the decrease in financial burden on the person receiving child support.

(c) The best interests of the child and what is equitable between the parties.

(4) The burden of proof is on the person seeking the credit pursuant to this Subsection.

(5) Worksheet A reproduced in R.S. 9:315.20, or a substantially similar form adopted by local court rule, shall be used to determine child support in accordance with this Subsection.

EFFECT OF SHARED CUSTODIAL ARRANGEMENT

If you have a joint custody order wherein you have the physical custody approximately 50% of the time, then it likely will be defined as having "Shared Custody." Under a "Shared Custody" order, Worksheet "B" provided below is used in the child support calculation.

LSA-R.S. 9:315.9 Effect of shared custodial arrangement

A. (1) "Shared custody" means a joint custody order in which each parent has physical custody of the child for an approximately equal amount of time.

(2) If the joint custody order provides for shared custody, the basic child support obligation shall first be multiplied by one and one-half and then divided between the parents in proportion to their respective adjusted gross incomes.

(3) Each parent's theoretical child support obligation shall then be cross multiplied by the actual percentage of time the child spends with the other party to determine the basic child support obligation based on the amount of time spent with the other party.

(4) Each parent's proportionate share of work-related net child care costs and extraordinary adjustments to the schedule shall be added to the amount calculated under Paragraph (3) of this Subsection.

(5) Each parent's proportionate share of any direct payments ordered to be made on behalf of the child for net child care costs, the cost of health insurance premiums, extraordinary medical expenses, or other extraordinary expenses shall be deducted from the amount calculated under Paragraph (3) of this Subsection.

(6) The parent owing the greater amount of child support shall owe to the other parent the difference between the two amounts as a child support obligation. The amount owed shall not be higher than the amount which that parent would have owed if he or she were a domiciliary parent.

B. Worksheet B reproduced in R.S. 9:315.20, or a substantially similar form adopted by local court rule, shall be used to determine child support in accordance with this Subsection.

EFFECT OF SPLIT CUSTODIAL ARRANGEMENT

If you have a sole custody order or are the domiciliary parent of at least one child, then it likely will be defined as having "Split Custody" for purposes of child support calculation. Under a "Split Custody" order, Worksheet "A" provided below is used in the child support calculation.

LA-R.S. 9:315.10 Effect of split custodial arrangement

A. (1) "Split custody" means that each party is the sole custodial or domiciliary parent of at least one child to whom support is due.

(2) If the custody order provides for split custody, each parent shall compute a total child support obligation for the child or children in the custody of the other parent, based on a calculation pursuant to this Section.

(3) The amount determined under Paragraph (2) of this Subsection shall be a theoretical support obligation owed to each parent.

(4) The parent owing the greater amount of child support shall owe to the other parent the difference between the two amounts as a child support obligation.

B. Worksheet A reproduced in R.S. 9:315.20, or a substantially similar form adopted by local court rule, shall be used by each parent to determine child support in accordance with this Section.

VOLUNTARILY UNEMPLOYED OR UNDEREMPLOYED PARTY

It is quite common for a parent to try to alleviate the child support financial burden by loosing a job, working less hours, manipulating the timing of bonuses and raises, and the like, for the primary purpose of establishing a lower gross income and thus paying less child support. The courts and the Louisiana legislature have recognized this problem. LA-R.S. 9:315.11 addresses this common tactic. The courts are allowed to impute income on a parent who voluntarily becomes unemployed or underemployed. In other words, the court will calculate the payor parent's income at a level determined to be appropriate had the parent not become voluntarily unemployed or underemployed. One of the best ways to prove voluntary unemployment is through the testimony of co-workers and employers as well as through payroll records.

LA-R.S. 9:315.11 Voluntarily unemployed or underemployed party

If a party is voluntarily unemployed or underemployed, child support shall be calculated based on a determination of his or her income earning potential, unless the party is physically or mentally incapacitated, or is caring for a child of the parties under the age of five years.

SECOND JOBS AND OVERTIME

LA-R.S. 9:315.12 Second jobs and overtime

The court may consider the interests of a subsequent family as a defense in an action to modify an existing child support order when the obligor has taken a second job or works overtime to provide for a subsequent family. However, the obligor bears the burden of proof in establishing that the additional income is used to provide for the subsequent family.

AMOUNTS NOT SET FORTH IN OR EXCEEDING THE SCHEDULE

LA-R.S. 9:315.13 Amounts not set forth in or exceeding schedule

A. If the combined adjusted gross income of the parties falls between two amounts shown in the schedule contained in R.S. 9:315.19, the basic child support obligation shall be based on an extrapolation between the two amounts.

B. If the combined adjusted gross income of the parties exceeds the highest level specified in the schedule contained in R.S. 9:315.19, the court shall use its discretion in setting the amount of the basic child support obligation in accordance with the best interest of the child and the circumstances of each parent as provided in Civil Code Article 141, but in no event shall it be less than the highest amount set forth in the schedule.

LA-R.S. 9:315.14 Mandatory minimum child support award

In no event shall the court set an award of child support less than one hundred dollars, except in cases involving shared or split custody as provided in R.S. 9:315.9 and 315.10.

SCHEDULE FOR CHILD SUPPORT

LA-R.S. 9:315.18 Schedule; information

A. The amounts set forth in the schedule in R.S. 9:315.19 presume that the custodial or domiciliary party has the right to claim the federal and state tax dependency deductions and any earned income credit. However, the claiming of dependents for federal and state income tax purposes shall be as provided in Subsection B of this Section.

B. (1) The non-domiciliary party whose child support obligation is equal to or greater than fifty percent and equal to or less than seventy percent of the total child support obligation shall be entitled to claim the federal and state tax dependency deductions if, after a contradictory motion, the judge finds both of the following:

(a) No arrearages are owed by the obligor.

(b) The right to claim the dependency deductions or, in the case of multiple children, a part thereof, would substantially benefit the non-domiciliary party without significantly harming the domiciliary party.

(2) The child support order shall:

(a) Specify the years in which the party is entitled to claim such deductions.

(b) Require the domiciliary party to timely execute

all forms required by the Internal Revenue Service authorizing the non-domiciliary party to claim such deductions.

C. The non-domiciliary party whose child support obligation exceeds seventy percent of the total child support obligation shall be entitled to claim the federal and state tax dependency deductions every year if no arrearages are owed by the obligor.

D. The party who receives the benefit of the exemption for such tax year shall not be considered as having received payment of a thing not due if the dependency deduction allocation is not maintained by the taxing authorities.

LA-R.S. 9:315.19 Schedule for support

The schedule of support to be used for determining the basic child support obligation is as follows:

LOUISIANA CHILD SUPPORT GUIDELINE SCHEDULE OF BASIC CHILD SUPPORT OBLIGATIONS

COMBINED ADJUSTED MONTHLY GROSS INCOME (TOTAL)	ONE CHILD	TWO CHILDREN (TOTAL)	THREE CHILDREN (TOTAL)	FOUR CHILDREN (TOTAL)	FIVE CHILDREN (TOTAL)	SIX OR MORE CHILDREN
600.00	100	100	100	100	100	100
650.00	102	103	104	106	107	108
700.00	136	138	139	141	142	144
750.00	165	172	174	176	178	179
800.00	174	206	208	211	213	215
850.00	182	240	243	245	248	251
900.00	189	274	277	280	283	286
950.00	197	305	310	313	317	320
1000.00	203	315	339	342	346	350
1050.00	210	325	367	371	375	379
1100.00	216	335	396	400	405	409
1150.00	222	345	425	429	434	439
1200.00	229	354	444	458	463	468
1250.00	235	364	456	487	493	498
1300.00	241	374	469	516	522	528
1350.00	248	384	481	542	551	557
1400.00	254	394	494	556	581	587
1450.00	260	404	506	570	610	617
1500.00	267	414	519	584	637	646
1550.00	273	424	531	598	653	676
1600.00	281	435	545	614	670	717
1650.00	288	446	560	630	688	736
1700.00	295	458	574	647	705	755
1750.00	303	469	588	663	723	774
1800.00	310	481	603	679	741	792
1850.00	317	492	617	695	758	811
1900.00	325	503	631	711	776	830
1950.00	331	513	643	724	790	846
2000.00	337	522	655	737	805	861
2050.00	343	532	667	751	819	877
2100.00	349	541	679	764	834	892
2150.00	355	551	691	778	849	908
2200.00	361	561	703	792	864	924
2250.00	368	570	715	805	878	940
2300.00	374	580	727	819	893	956
2350.00	380	590	739	832	908	972
2400.00	386	600	751	846	923	988
2450.00	392	609	763	860	938	1004
2500.00	399	619	776	873	953	1020
2550.00	405	629	788	887	968	1035
2600.00	411	638	800	901	983	1051
2650.00	417	648	812	914	998	1067
2700.00	424	658	824	928	1013	1083
2750.00	430	668	836	942	1028	1099
2800.00	436	677	848	955	1042	1115
2850.00	442	687	860	969	1057	1131
2900.00	448	697	872	983	1072	1147
2950.00	455	706	885	996	1087	1163
3000.00	461	716	897	1010	1102	1179
3050.00	467	726	909	1024	1117	1195
3100.00	473	736	921	1037	1132	1211
3150.00	479	745	933	1051	1147	1227
3200.00	486	755	945	1065	1162	1243
3250.00	492	765	957	1078	1177	1259
3300.00	498	774	969	1092	1192	1275
3350.00	504	784	981	1106	1206	1291
3400.00	510	794	994	1119	1221	1307
3450.00	517	804	1006	1133	1236	1323
3500.00	523	813	1018	1146	1251	1339

3550.00	529	823	1030	1160	1266	1355
3600.00	535	833	1042	1174	1281	1371
3650.00	542	842	1054	1187	1296	1387
3700.00	548	852	1066	1201	1311	1402
3750.00	554	862	1078	1215	1326	1418
3800.00	560	872	1090	1228	1341	1434
3850.00	566	881	1103	1242	1356	1450
3900.00	573	891	1115	1256	1371	1466
3950.00	579	901	1127	1269	1385	1482
4000.00	585	910	1139	1283	1400	1498
4050.00	590	919	1149	1295	1414	1512
4100.00	596	927	1160	1307	1427	1526
4150.00	601	936	1170	1319	1440	1540
4200.00	607	944	1181	1331	1452	1553
4250.00	612	953	1191	1343	1465	1567
4300.00	618	961	1202	1355	1478	1581
4350.00	623	970	1212	1367	1491	1595
4400.00	629	978	1223	1379	1504	1609
4450.00	634	987	1234	1391	1517	1623
4500.00	640	995	1244	1403	1530	1637
4550.00	645	1003	1255	1415	1543	1650
4600.00	651	1012	1265	1426	1556	1664
4650.00	656	1020	1276	1438	1569	1678
4700.00	662	1029	1286	1450	1582	1692
4750.00	667	1037	1297	1462	1595	1706
4800.00	673	1046	1307	1474	1608	1720
4850.00	678	1054	1318	1486	1621	1734
4900.00	684	1063	1328	1498	1634	1747
4950.00	689	1071	1339	1510	1647	1761
5000.00	695	1079	1349	1522	1660	1775
5050.00	700	1088	1360	1534	1673	1789
5100.00	706	1096	1370	1545	1686	1803
5150.00	711	1105	1381	1557	1699	1817
5200.00	717	1113	1391	1569	1712	1831
5250.00	722	1122	1402	1581	1725	1844
5300.00	728	1130	1413	1593	1738	1858
5350.00	733	1139	1423	1605	1751	1872
5400.00	738	1146	1432	1616	1763	1884
5450.00	743	1153	1441	1626	1774	1896
5500.00	748	1160	1450	1636	1785	1908
5550.00	752	1167	1459	1646	1796	1920
5600.00	757	1175	1468	1657	1807	1932
5650.00	762	1182	1478	1667	1819	1944
5700.00	767	1189	1487	1677	1830	1956
5750.00	771	1196	1496	1687	1841	1968
5800.00	776	1203	1505	1698	1852	1979
5850.00	781	1211	1514	1708	1863	1991
5900.00	785	1218	1523	1718	1875	2003
5950.00	790	1225	1532	1728	1886	2015
6000.00	795	1232	1541	1739	1897	2027
6050.00	800	1240	1550	1749	1908	2039
6100.00	804	1247	1559	1759	1919	2051
6150.00	809	1254	1568	1769	1931	2063
6200.00	814	1261	1577	1780	1942	2075
6250.00	819	1269	1587	1790	1953	2087
6300.00	823	1276	1596	1800	1964	2099
6350.00	828	1283	1605	1810	1975	2111
6400.00	833	1290	1614	1820	1987	2123
6450.00	838	1297	1623	1831	1998	2135
6500.00	842	1305	1632	1841	2009	2147
6550.00	847	1312	1641	1851	2020	2159
6600.00	852	1319	1650	1861	2031	2171
6650.00	857	1326	1659	1872	2043	2183
6700.00	861	1334	1668	1882	2054	2195
6750.00	866	1341	1677	1892	2065	2207
6800.00	871	1348	1687	1902	2076	2219
6850.00	875	1355	1696	1913	2087	2231

6900.00	879	1361	1703	1921	2096	2240
6950.00	883	1366	1710	1928	2105	2249
7000.00	886	1372	1717	1936	2113	2259
7050.00	889	1378	1725	1944	2122	2268
7100.00	893	1383	1732	1951	2130	2277
7150.00	896	1389	1739	1959	2139	2286
7200.00	900	1394	1746	1967	2147	2295
7250.00	903	1400	1753	1974	2156	2305
7300.00	906	1406	1760	1982	2164	2314
7350.00	910	1411	1767	1990	2173	2323
7400.00	913	1417	1774	1997	2181	2332
7450.00	916	1422	1781	2005	2189	2342
7500.00	920	1428	1788	2013	2198	2351
7550.00	923	1434	1795	2020	2206	2360
7600.00	927	1439	1802	2028	2215	2369
7650.00	930	1445	1809	2036	2223	2378
7700.00	933	1450	1816	2043	2232	2388
7750.00	937	1456	1824	2051	2240	2397
7800.00	940	1462	1831	2059	2243	2406
7850.00	944	1467	1838	2066	2246	2409
7900.00	947	1473	1845	2069	2249	2412
7950.00	950	1478	1852	2072	2252	2415
8000.00	954	1484	1859	2075	2255	2418
8050.00	957	1490	1866	2078	2258	2421
8100.00	960	1493	1871	2081	2261	2424
8150.00	962	1497	1875	2084	2264	2427
8200.00	965	1501	1880	2087	2267	2430
8250.00	967	1505	1882	2090	2270	2433
8300.00	970	1509	1884	2093	2273	2436
8350.00	972	1512	1886	2096	2276	2439
8400.00	975	1516	1888	2099	2279	2442
8450.00	977	1520	1890	2102	2282	2445
8500.00	980	1523	1892	2105	2285	2448
8550.00	982	1526	1894	2108	2288	2451
8600.00	985	1529	1896	2111	2291	2454
8650.00	987	1532	1898	2114	2294	2457
8700.00	990	1535	1900	2117	2297	2460
8750.00	992	1538	1902	2120	2300	2463
8800.00	995	1541	1904	2123	2303	2466
8850.00	997	1544	1906	2126	2306	2469
8900.00	1000	1547	1908	2129	2309	2472
8950.00	1003	1550	1910	2132	2312	2475
9000.00	1005	1553	1912	2135	2315	2478
9050.00	1008	1556	1914	2138	2318	2481
9100.00	1011	1559	1916	2141	2321	2484
9150.00	1013	1562	1918	2144	2324	2487
9200.00	1016	1565	1920	2147	2327	2490
9250.00	1019	1568	1922	2150	2330	2493
9300.00	1022	1571	1924	2153	2333	2496
9350.00	1024	1574	1926	2156	2336	2499
9400.00	1028	1577	1928	2159	2339	2502
9450.00	1033	1580	1930	2162	2342	2505
9500.00	1038	1583	1932	2165	2345	2508
9550.00	1043	1586	1934	2168	2348	2511
9600.00	1048	1589	1936	2171	2351	2514
9650.00	1053	1592	1938	2174	2354	2517
9700.00	1058	1595	1940	2177	2357	2520
9750.00	1063	1598	1942	2180	2360	2523
9800.00	1068	1601	1944	2183	2363	2526
9850.00	1073	1604	1946	2186	2366	2529
9900.00	1078	1607	1948	2189	2369	2532
9950.00	1083	1610	1950	2192	2372	2535
10000.00	1088	1613	1952	2195	2375	2538
10050.00	1095	1615	1954	2197	2377	2540
10100.00	1102	1617	1956	2199	2379	2542
10150.00	1109	1619	1958	2201	2381	2544
10200.00	1115	1621	1960	2203	2383	2546

10250.00	1119	1623	1962	2205	2385	2548
10300.00	1123	1625	1964	2207	2387	2550
10350.00	1127	1630	1966	2209	2389	2552
10400.00	1131	1636	1968	2211	2391	2554
10450.00	1135	1642	1970	2213	2393	2556
10500.00	1138	1647	1972	2215	2395	2558
10550.00	1142	1653	1974	2217	2397	2560
10600.00	1146	1659	1976	2219	2399	2562
10650.00	1150	1665	1978	2221	2400	2564
10700.00	1154	1670	1982	2223	2402	2566
10750.00	1158	1676	1984	2225	2404	2568
10800.00	1162	1682	1986	2227	2406	2570
10850.00	1166	1687	1988	2229	2408	2572
10900.00	1170	1693	1994	2231	2410	2574
10950.00	1174	1698	2001	2233	2412	2576
11000.00	1178	1704	2008	2235	2414	2578
11050.00	1182	1710	2014	2237	2416	2582
11100.00	1186	1715	2021	2239	2421	2590
11150.00	1190	1721	2027	2241	2429	2599
11200.00	1194	1727	2034	2248	2436	2607
11250.00	1197	1732	2041	2255	2444	2616
11300.00	1201	1738	2047	2262	2452	2624
11350.00	1205	1744	2054	2270	2460	2632
11400.00	1209	1749	2061	2277	2468	2641
11450.00	1213	1755	2067	2284	2476	2649
11500.00	1217	1760	2073	2291	2483	2657
11550.00	1220	1765	2079	2298	2491	2665
11600.00	1224	1771	2085	2304	2498	2673
11650.00	1228	1776	2092	2311	2505	2681
11700.00	1231	1781	2098	2318	2513	2689
11750.00	1235	1786	2104	2325	2520	2696
11800.00	1239	1791	2110	2331	2527	2704
11850.00	1242	1797	2116	2338	2535	2712
11900.00	1246	1802	2122	2345	2542	2720
11950.00	1249	1807	2128	2352	2549	2728
12000.00	1253	1812	2134	2358	2557	2735
12050.00	1257	1818	2140	2365	2564	2743
12100.00	1260	1823	2147	2372	2571	2751
12150.00	1264	1828	2153	2379	2578	2759
12200.00	1268	1833	2159	2385	2586	2767
12250.00	1271	1838	2165	2392	2593	2775
12300.00	1275	1844	2171	2399	2600	2782
12350.00	1278	1849	2177	2406	2608	2790
12400.00	1282	1854	2183	2412	2615	2798
12450.00	1286	1859	2189	2419	2622	2806
12500.00	1289	1864	2195	2426	2630	2814
12550.00	1293	1870	2202	2433	2637	2822
12600.00	1297	1875	2208	2439	2644	2829
12650.00	1300	1880	2214	2446	2652	2837
12700.00	1304	1885	2220	2453	2659	2845
12750.00	1307	1891	2226	2460	2666	2853
12800.00	1311	1896	2232	2466	2674	2861
12850.00	1315	1901	2238	2473	2681	2869
12900.00	1318	1906	2244	2480	2688	2876
12950.00	1322	1911	2250	2487	2696	2884
13000.00	1326	1917	2257	2493	2703	2892
13050.00	1329	1922	2263	2500	2710	2900
13100.00	1333	1927	2269	2507	2718	2908
13150.00	1336	1932	2275	2514	2725	2916
13200.00	1340	1937	2281	2520	2732	2923
13250.00	1344	1943	2287	2527	2740	2931
13300.00	1347	1948	2293	2534	2747	2939
13350.00	1351	1953	2299	2541	2754	2947
13400.00	1355	1958	2305	2547	2761	2955
13450.00	1358	1964	2312	2554	2769	2963
13500.00	1362	1969	2318	2561	2776	2970
13550.00	1365	1974	2324	2568	2783	2978

13600.00	1369	1979	2330	2574	2791	2986
13650.00	1373	1984	2336	2581	2798	2994
13700.00	1376	1990	2342	2588	2805	3002
13750.00	1380	1995	2348	2595	2813	3010
13800.00	1384	2000	2354	2601	2820	3017
13850.00	1387	2005	2360	2608	2827	3025
13900.00	1391	2011	2367	2615	2835	3033
13950.00	1394	2016	2373	2622	2842	3041
14000.00	1398	2021	2379	2629	2849	3049
14050.00	1402	2026	2385	2635	2857	3057
14100.00	1405	2031	2391	2642	2864	3064
14150.00	1409	2037	2397	2649	2871	3072
14200.00	1413	2042	2403	2656	2879	3080
14250.00	1416	2047	2409	2662	2886	3088
14300.00	1420	2052	2415	2669	2893	3096
14350.00	1423	2057	2422	2676	2901	3104
14400.00	1427	2063	2428	2683	2908	3111
14450.00	1431	2068	2434	2689	2915	3119
14500.00	1434	2073	2440	2696	2922	3127
14550.00	1438	2078	2446	2703	2930	3135
14600.00	1442	2084	2452	2710	2937	3143
14650.00	1445	2089	2458	2716	2944	3151
14700.00	1449	2094	2464	2723	2952	3158
14750.00	1452	2099	2470	2730	2959	3166
14800.00	1456	2104	2476	2737	2966	3174
14850.00	1460	2110	2483	2743	2974	3182
14900.00	1463	2115	2489	2750	2981	3190
14950.00	1467	2120	2495	2757	2988	3198
15000.00	1471	2125	2501	2764	2996	3205
15050.00	1474	2130	2507	2770	3003	3213
15100.00	1478	2136	2513	2777	3010	3221
15150.00	1481	2141	2519	2784	3018	3229
15200.00	1485	2146	2525	2791	3025	3237
15250.00	1489	2151	2531	2797	3032	3245
15300.00	1492	2157	2538	2804	3040	3252
15350.00	1496	2162	2544	2811	3047	3260
15400.00	1500	2167	2550	2818	3054	3268
15450.00	1503	2172	2556	2824	3062	3276
15500.00	1507	2177	2562	2831	3069	3284
15550.00	1510	2183	2568	2838	3076	3292
15600.00	1514	2188	2574	2845	3083	3299
15650.00	1518	2193	2580	2851	3091	3307
15700.00	1521	2198	2586	2858	3098	3315
15750.00	1525	2203	2593	2865	3105	3323
15800.00	1529	2209	2599	2872	3113	3331
15850.00	1532	2214	2605	2878	3120	3338
15900.00	1536	2219	2611	2885	3127	3346
15950.00	1539	2224	2617	2892	3135	3354
16000.00	1543	2230	2623	2899	3142	3362
16050.00	1547	2235	2629	2905	3149	3370
16100.00	1550	2240	2635	2912	3157	3378
16150.00	1554	2245	2641	2919	3164	3385
16200.00	1558	2250	2648	2926	3171	3393
16250.00	1561	2256	2654	2932	3179	3401
16300.00	1565	2261	2660	2939	3186	3409
16350.00	1568	2266	2666	2946	3193	3417
16400.00	1572	2271	2672	2953	3201	3425
16450.00	1576	2277	2678	2959	3208	3432
16500.00	1579	2282	2684	2966	3215	3440
16550.00	1583	2287	2690	2973	3223	3448
16600.00	1587	2292	2696	2980	3230	3456
16650.00	1590	2297	2703	2986	3237	3464
16700.00	1594	2303	2709	2993	3245	3472
16750.00	1597	2308	2715	3000	3252	3479
16800.00	1601	2313	2721	3007	3259	3487
16850.00	1605	2318	2727	3013	3266	3495
16900.00	1608	2323	2733	3020	3274	3503

16950.00	1612	2329	2739	3027	3281	3511
17000.00	1616	2334	2745	3034	3288	3519
17050.00	1619	2339	2751	3040	3296	3526
17100.00	1623	2344	2758	3047	3303	3534
17150.00	1626	2350	2764	3054	3310	3542
17200.00	1630	2355	2770	3061	3318	3550
17250.00	1634	2360	2776	3067	3325	3558
17300.00	1637	2365	2782	3074	3332	3566
17350.00	1641	2370	2788	3081	3340	3573
17400.00	1645	2376	2794	3088	3347	3581
17450.00	1648	2381	2800	3094	3354	3589
17500.00	1652	2386	2806	3101	3362	3597
17550.00	1655	2391	2813	3108	3369	3605
17600.00	1659	2396	2819	3115	3376	3613
17650.00	1663	2402	2825	3121	3384	3620
17700.00	1666	2407	2831	3128	3391	3628
17750.00	1670	2412	2837	3135	3398	3636
17800.00	1674	2417	2843	3142	3406	3644
17850.00	1677	2423	2849	3148	3413	3652
17900.00	1681	2428	2855	3155	3420	3660
17950.00	1684	2433	2861	3162	3427	3667
18000.00	1688	2438	2868	3169	3435	3675
18050.00	1692	2443	2874	3175	3442	3683
18100.00	1695	2449	2880	3182	3449	3691
18150.00	1699	2454	2886	3189	3457	3699
18200.00	1703	2459	2892	3196	3464	3707
18250.00	1706	2464	2898	3202	3471	3714
18300.00	1710	2469	2904	3209	3479	3722
18350.00	1713	2475	2910	3216	3486	3730
18400.00	1717	2480	2916	3223	3493	3738
18450.00	1721	2485	2923	3229	3501	3746
18500.00	1724	2490	2929	3236	3508	3754
18550.00	1728	2496	2935	3243	3515	3761
18600.00	1732	2501	2941	3250	3523	3769
18650.00	1735	2506	2947	3256	3530	3777
18700.00	1739	2511	2953	3263	3537	3785
18750.00	1742	2516	2959	3270	3545	3793
18800.00	1746	2522	2965	3277	3552	3801
18850.00	1750	2527	2971	3283	3559	3808
18900.00	1753	2532	2978	3290	3567	3816
18950.00	1757	2537	2984	3297	3574	3824
19000.00	1761	2543	2990	3304	3581	3832
19050.00	1764	2548	2996	3310	3589	3840
19100.00	1768	2553	3002	3317	3596	3848
19150.00	1771	2558	3008	3324	3603	3855
19200.00	1775	2563	3014	3331	3610	3863
19250.00	1779	2569	3020	3337	3618	3871
19300.00	1782	2574	3026	3344	3625	3879
19350.00	1786	2579	3033	3351	3632	3887
19400.00	1790	2584	3039	3358	3640	3895
19450.00	1793	2589	3045	3364	3647	3902
19500.00	1797	2595	3051	3371	3654	3910
19550.00	1800	2600	3057	3378	3662	3918
19600.00	1804	2605	3063	3385	3669	3926
19650.00	1808	2610	3069	3391	3676	3934
19700.00	1811	2616	3075	3398	3684	3942
19750.00	1815	2621	3081	3405	3691	3949
19800.00	1819	2626	3088	3412	3698	3957
19850.00	1822	2631	3094	3418	3706	3965
19900.00	1826	2636	3100	3425	3713	3973
19950.00	1829	2642	3106	3432	3720	3981
20000.00	1833	2647	3112	3439	3728	3988

CHILD SUPPORT OBLIGATION WORKSHEET "A"

```
Court _____ Parish _____
                              Louisiana
Case Number _____ Div/CtRm _____

_____ and _____
        Petitioner                          Respondent

Children            Date of Birth  Children              Da
                    te of Birth

_____   _____

                              _____

_____   _____

                              _____

_____   _____

                              _____

                              ---------------------------------------
                  -----------
                              : A. Petitioner : B. Respondent :
                  C. Combined
-----------------------------------------------------------------------
                  -----------
1. MONTHLY GROSS INCOME (R.S.    : $_____ : $ _____ :
                                 /////////
   9:315.2(A))                   :                :            :
                                 /////////
      a. Preexisting child support   : -_____ : -
                      _____ : /////////
      payment.                   :                :            :
                                 /////////
      b. Preexisting spousal support : -_____ : -
                      _____ : /////////
      payment.                   :                :            :
                                 /////////
-----------------------------------------------------------------------
                  -----------
2. MONTHLY ADJUSTED GROSS INCOME  : $             : $          :
                                 /////////
   (Line 1 minus 1a and 1b).     :                :            :
                                 /////////
-----------------------------------------------------------------------
                  -----------
3. COMBINED MONTHLY ADJUSTED      :   ///////////// :   ///////////// :
                                 $
   GROSS INCOME (Line 2 Column    :   ///////////// :   ///////////// :
   A plus Line 2 Column B).       :   ///////////// :   ///////////// :
   (R.S. 9:315.2(C))              :   ///////////// :   ///////////// :
-----------------------------------------------------------------------
                  -----------
4. PERCENTAGE SHARE OF INCOME     :              % :            % :
                                 ////////
   (Line 2 divided by line 3).    :                :            :
                                 ////////
   (R.S. 9:315.2(C))              :                :            :
                                 ////////
-----------------------------------------------------------------------
                  -----------
5. BASIC CHILD SUPPORT OBLIGATION :   ///////////// :   ///////////// :
                                 $
   (Compare line 3 to Child       :   ///////////// :   ///////////// :
   Support Schedule). (R.S.       :   ///////////// :   ///////////// :
   9:315.2(D))                    :   ///////////// :   ///////////// :
-----------------------------------------------------------------------
```

```
                 -----------
    a. Net Child Care Costs (Cost :   /////////// :   //////////// :
                         +
        minus Federal Tax       :   /////////// :   //////////// :
        Credit). (R.S. 9:315.3) :   /////////// :   //////////// :
    b. Child's Health Insurance :   /////////// :   //////////// :
                         +
        Premium Cost. (R.S.     :   /////////// :   //////////// :
        9:315.4)                :   /////////// :   //////////// :
    c. Extraordinary Medical    :   /////////// :   //////////// :
                         +
        Expenses (Uninsured     :   /////////// :   //////////// :
        Only). (Agreed to by    :   /////////// :   //////////// :
        parties or by order of  :   /////////// :   //////////// :
        the court). (R.S.       :   /////////// :   //////////// :
        9:315.5)                :   /////////// :   //////////// :
    d. Extraordinary Expenses   :   /////////// :   //////////// :
                         +
        (Agreed to by parties or :  /////////// :   //////////// :
        by order of the court). :   /////////// :   //////////// :
        (R.S. 9:315.6)          :   /////////// :   //////////// :
    e. Optional. Minus          :   /////////// :   //////////// :
                         -
        extraordinary adjustments : /////////// :   //////////// :
        (Child's income if      :   /////////// :   //////////// :
        applicable). (R.S.      :   /////////// :   //////////// :
        9:315.7)                :   /////////// :   //////////// :
----------------------------------------------------------------------
                 -----------
6. TOTAL CHILD SUPPORT OBLIGATION :  /////////// :   /////////// :
                         $
    (Add lines 5, 5a, 5b, 5c,   :   /////////// :   /////////// :
    and 5d; Subtract line 5e).  :   /////////// :   /////////// :
    (R.S. 9:315.8)              :   /////////// :   /////////// :
----------------------------------------------------------------------
                 -----------
7. EACH PARTY'S CHILD SUPPORT     : $               : $           :
                         /////////
    OBLIGATION (Multiply line 4 :                   :             :
                         /////////
    times line 6 for each       :                   :             :
                         /////////
    parent).                    :                   :             :
                         /////////
----------------------------------------------------------------------
                 -----------
    8. DIRECT PAYMENTS made by the  :  /////////// : -
                            : /////////
    noncustodial parent on      :   /////////// :             :
                         /////////
    behalf of the child for     :   /////////// :             :
                         /////////
                         work-
related net child care  :  /////////// :              :  //////// 
                         /
    costs, health insurance     :   /////////// :             :
                         /////////
    premiums, extraordinary     :   /////////// :             :
                         /////////
    medical expenses, or        :   /////////// :             :
                         /////////
    extraordinary expenses.     :   /////////// :             :
                         /////////
----------------------------------------------------------------------
                 -----------
9. RECOMMENDED CHILD SUPPORT      :   /////////// : $           :
                         /////////
```

```
     ORDER (Subtract line 8 from  :  ///////////  :                    :
                                     ////////
     line 7).                        :  ///////////  :                :
                                     ////////
------------------------------------------------------------------------
                           -----------



------------------------------------------------------------------------
                           -----------
Comments, calculations, or rebuttals to schedule or adjustments if m
                           ade under 8
   above or if ordering a credit for a joint custodial arrangement:

Prepared by _____  Date _____
                           _____
```

CHILD SUPPORT OBLIGATION WORKSHEET "B"

Obligation Worksheet B
(The worksheet for calculation of the total child support obligation
under R.S.9:315.9)

Court _____ Parish _____

 Louisiana

Case Number _____ Div/CtRm _____

_____

_____ and _____

_____

Petitioner   Respondent

Children   Date of Birth Children   Da
te of Birth

_____   _____

_____

_____   _____

_____

_____   _____

_____

                              : A. Petitioner : B. Respondent :
C. Combined

----

1. MONTHLY GROSS INCOME (R.S. : $_____ $ _____ :
////////

       9:315.2(A))   :   :   :
////////

                                                :

    a. Preexisting child support : -_____ : -
_____   ////////

```
         payment.                  :              :              :
   /////////


                                                                  :

     b. Preexisting spousal        : -_____ : -
_____      /////////

        support payment.           :              :              :
   /////////


                                                                  :
------------------------------------------------------------------
-----------
2.  MONTHLY ADJUSTED GROSS INCOME   $              : $            :
   /////////

        (Line 1 minus 1a and 1b).   :              :              :
   /////////


                                    :
------------------------------------------------------------------
-----------
3.  COMBINED MONTHLY ADJUSTED        :  ///////////  :  ///////////  :
$

        GROSS INCOME (Line 2 Column  :  ///////////  :  ///////////  :
        A plus Line 2 Column B).     :  ///////////  :  ///////////  :
        (R.S.  9:315.2(C))           :  ///////////  :  ///////////  :
------------------------------------------------------------------
-----------
4.  PERCENTAGE SHARE OF INCOME       :              % :              % :
   /////////

        (Line 2 divided by line 3). :              :              :
   /////////

        (R.S.  9:315.2(C))           :              :              :
   /////////
------------------------------------------------------------------
-----------
5.  BASIC CHILD SUPPORT              :  ///////////   ///////////  :
$
```

```
        OBLIGATION (Compare line 3   :   ///////////  :   ///////////  :
        to Child Support Schedule). :   ///////////  :   ///////////  :
        (R.S. 9:315.2(D))            :   ///////////  :   ///////////  :
                                     :                :
--------------------------------------------------------------------------
-----------
6.  SHARED CUSTODY BASIC             :   ///////////  :   ///////////  :
$
        OBLIGATION (Line 5 times     :   ///////////  :   ///////////  :
        1.5) (R.S. 9:315.9( A)(2))   :   ///////////  :   ///////////  :
--------------------------------------------------------------------------
-----------
7.  EACH PARTY'S THEORETICAL         : $              : $
  ////////
        CHILD SUPPORT OBLIGATION     :                :              :
  ////////
        (Multiply line 4 times line  :                :              :
  ////////
        6 for each party)(R.S.       :                :              :
  ////////
        9:315.9(A)(2))DIAGONAL       :                :              :
  1 //////
        ARROWS LINK ITEMS 7 AND 8    :                :              :
  ////////
                                                      :
--------------------------------------------------------------------------
-----------
8.  PERCENTAGE with each party                        % :            % :
  ////////
        (Use actual percentage of    :                :              :
  ////////
        time spent with each party,  :                :              :
  ////////
        if percentage is not 50%)    :                :              :
```

```
/////////
      (R.S. 9:315.9(A)(3))          :              :              :
 /////////

                                     :

---------------------------------------------------------------------
-----------
9.  BASIC CHILD SUPPORT              : $             : $
 /////////
      OBLIGATION FOR TIME WITH       :              :              :
 /////////
      OTHER PARTY ( Cross            :              :              :
 /////////
      Multiply line 7 for each       :              :              :
 /////////
      party times line 8 for the     :              :              :
 /////////
      other party) (R.S.             :              :              :
 /////////
      9:315.9(A)(3)) (For Line 9     :              :              :
 /////////
      Column A, multiply Line 7      :              :              :
 /////////
      Column A times Line 8          :              :              :
 /////////
      Column B) (For Line 9          :              :              :
 /////////
      Column B, multiply Line 7      :              :              :
 /////////
      Column B times Line 8          :              :              :
 /////////
      Column A)                                                    :
---------------------------------------------------------------------
-----------
      a. Net Child Care Costs (Cost     /////////// :  /////////// :
```

+_____

minus Federal Tax	:	/////////// :	/////////// :
Credit). (R.S. 9:315.3)	:	/////////// :	/////////// :
	:		
b. Child's Health Insurance	:	/////////// :	/////////// :

+_____

Premium Cost. (R.S.	:	/////////// :	/////////// :
9:315.4)	:	/////////// :	/////////// :
c. Extraordinary Medical	:	/////////// :	///////////

+_____

Expenses (Uninsured	:	/////////// :	/////////// :
Only). (Agreed to by	:	/////////// :	/////////// :
parties or by order of	:	/////////// :	/////////// :
the court). (R.S.	:	/////////// :	/////////// :
9:315.5)	:	/////////// :	/////////// :
	:		
d. Extraordinary Expenses	:	/////////// :	/////////// :

+_____

(Agreed to by parties or	:	/////////// :	/////////// :
by order of the court).	:	/////////// :	/////////// :
(R.S. 9:315.6)	:	/////////// :	/////////// :
e. Optional. Minus	:	///////////	/////////// :

-_____

extraordinary	:	/////////// :	/////////// :
adjustments (Child's	:	/////////// :	/////////// :
income if applicable).	:	/////////// :	/////////// :
(R.S. 9:315.7)	:	/////////// :	/////////// :
	:		

----

10. TOTAL EXPENSES/EXTRAORDINARY	:	///////////	/////////// :
$			
ADJUSTMENTS (Add lines 9a,	:	/////////// :	/////////// :
9b, 9c, and 9d, Subtract	:	/////////// :	/////////// :

```
    line 9e)                        :   /////////// :   /////////// :
                                                         :

----------------------------------------------------------------------
-----------

11. EACH PARTY'S PROPORTIONATE       $            : $              :
   /////////

      SHARE of Expenses/            :            :              :
   /////////

      Extraordinary Adjustments    :            :              :
   /////////

      (Line 4 times line 10)       :            :              :
   /////////

      (R.S. 9:315.9(A)(4))         :            :              :
   /////////

                                                :

----------------------------------------------------------------------
-----------

12. DIRECT PAYMENTS made by        : -          : -
          :  /////////

      either party on behalf of    :            :              :
   /////////

      the child for work-
related :                :                     :  /////////

      net child care costs,        :            :              :
   /////////

      health insurance premiums,   :            :              :
   /////////

      extraordinary medical        :            :              :
   /////////

      expenses, or extraordinary   :            :              :
   /////////

      expenses. Deduct each        :            :              :
   /////////

      party's percentage share of :            :              :
```

////////

    the expense owed directly   :   :   :

////////

    to a third party. (R.S.   :   :   :

////////

    9:315.9(A)(5))   :   :   :

////////

----

13. EACH PARTY'S CHILD SUPPORT   : $ $:

////////

    OBLIGATION (Line 9 plus   :   :   :

////////

    line 11 and minus line 12) :   :   :

////////

    (R.S. 9:315.9(A)(4) and   :   :   :

////////

    (5))   :   :   :

////////

                           :

----

14. RECOMMENDED CHILD SUPPORT   : $: $:

////////

    ORDER (Subtract lesser   :   :   :

////////

    amount from greater amount :   :   :

61 //////

    in line 13 and place the   :   :   :

////////

    difference in the   :   :   :

////////

    appropriate column) (R.S.   :   :   :

////////

```
     9:315.9(A)(6))                    :                 :                    :

  ////////

  -----------------------------------------------------------------------

  -----------


  -----------------------------------------------------------------------

  ----------

  Comments, calculations, or rebuttals to schedule or adjustments:


  Prepared by _____  Date _____

  _____
```

WATCH FOR MANIPULATION
OF THE NUMBERS

Unfortunately, many lawyers may add "two plus two" and come up with "three." There are no national or statewide criteria on determining how much a person earns. Likewise, there no uniform standards regarding what period of time should be used to examine a parent's income. Many jobs are cyclical such as construction, lawn care, Christmas tree sales, etc.; hence, the more cyclical the business, the more important it is to have an examination of income over a twelve month or a greater period of time. Some courts will look at the income over several years. Tax returns may give insight as to whether a parent is manipulating his or her income.

CHECK THE CALCULATION
OF EACH PARENT'S INCOME

Be leery of anyone who quickly estimates and/or calculates what the other parent makes in an average month. People have wide and diverse payment methods. Many people get paid by the hour, by the week, by the job, every two weeks, get paid overtime, get reimbursed for travel expenses, have expense accounts, etc.

Since child support guidelines provide formulas for calculations based on average actual income and/or earnings capacity, the time period from which the "average" is taken becomes critical.

For example, if parent one ("Huey P.") earned the following income for the last year and one-half, the time period used to determine his average monthly income and/or earnings capacity could create significantly varied results.

Huey P.'s "Declared" Income:

Last year:	January	$3,000.00
	February	3,000.00
	March	3,000.00
	April	3,000.00
	May	3,000.00
	June	3,000.00
	July	3,000.00
	August	3,000.00
	September	3,000.00
	October	3,000.00
	November	3,000.00
	December	3,000.00
Bonus (Paid in December)		6,000.00
This year:	January	2,000.00
	February	2,000.00
	March	2,000.00
	April	2,000.00
	May	2,000.00
	June	2,000.00

According to the above example, Huey P. made $42,000 last year. If your attorney did not discover that Huey P. made a $6,000.00 bonus, then he may incorrectly believe that Huey P.'s income last year was only $36,000. Additionally, if your attorney only calculated Huey P.'s average income based on his recent pay stub for the current year, your attorney would assume that Huey P. made an average of only $2,000.00 per month.

If your attorney calculates Huey P.'s income based on last year's income of $42,000, Huey P.'s average monthly declared income would be $3,500.

If your attorney calculates Huey P.'s income based on the last eighteen months, Huey P.'s average monthly declared income would be $3,000.

As you can see from the above example, lawyers can use the figures that are available (through proper discovery) and come up with entirely different answers to the question of what a parent's monthly income is. Have a talk with your attorney and ask him how he is calculating the declared income of each parent.

Instruct your attorney to subpoena the other parent's federal tax returns (and W-2 and/or 1099) for the past several years, as well as the payroll records and personnel files from his employer(s).

(Sample Questions: Did your attorney know that Huey P. would receive a bonus and reimbursement for travel expenses at the end of the year? Did your attorney know that Huey P. made an arrangement with his boss to defer his earned compensation until after the court resolved the child support issues?)

THERE ARE 4.3 WEEKS IN EACH MONTH

1.   Use the "4.3 Factor" when calculating a parent's income. Mistakes are continually made in calculating a parent's income by the assumption that there are four weeks in a month. There are not. Each year contains 52 weeks in a twelve-month period. Fifty-two divided by twelve equals 4.3. Hence, if the other parent is claiming to earn $1,000 per week, he may be declaring only $4,000 in income per month. His actual monthly income may be $4,300.

2.   Apply the "4.3 Factor" when calculating a child support award. Similar mistakes can be made in calculating the child support award. An award of $100 per week does not equal $400 per month. There are 52 weeks in a year. If child support is ordered at $100 per week, the recipient of the child support would get $5,200 per year. If child support is ordered at $400 per month, the recipient gets only $4,800 that year.

The above example shows how easy it can be for a party to manipulate the child support calculations using your state's guidelines.

Quick Facts

In last decade, women custodial parents received an average of $3,011 in annual child support payments. Male custodial parents received average annual child support payments of $2,292. (U.S. Census Bureau)

Your state's child support guidelines shall be presumed to be fair; however, most states allow for deviation from the standard guideline formulas based on the special circumstances of a parent or child.

DECLARED INCOME CAN BE MANIPULATED

It is worth repeating in this chapter: In order to effect the numbers used in the calculation of child support and/or alimony, a spouse may attempt to manipulate the numbers.

DECLARED INCOME CAN BE MANIPULATED BY:

1. Change his standard of living
2. Postpone salary increases
3. Delay bonuses
4. Encourage the other spouse to get a job or change jobs
5. Reduce the number of hours worked
6. Reduce overtime hours worked
7. Increase or decrease childcare expenses
8. Fail to report actual income earned in tax returns
9. Put assets/income in someone else's name (including new spouse)
10. Becoming "disabled"
11. Shelter money in corporations, partnerships, or trusts
12. Have personal expenses paid through family business
13. Get reimbursed by employer for personal expenses (i.e., auto expenses, meals, travel) and
14. Make misrepresentations to the court on required financial affidavit

LOOKING AT THE INCOME OF
YOUR EX'S NEW SPOUSE

States view your Ex's new spouse's income in various ways. Some states prohibit any consideration of this income in determining child support. Many states allow consideration of the income, but do not provide guidelines to the court on how to consider it. And states such as Louisiana allow the courts to consider the income of the new spouse <u>only indirectly to the extent that your Ex has shared living expenses with his new spouse and as such should have more disposable income available for child support.</u>

Generally, the new spouse's income will not be considered until or unless your attorney pushes for it (where allowed) and he or she has used discovery techniques to elicit the new spouse's income information.

LOOK AT FINANCIAL AFFIDAVITS
AND IN FORMA PAUPERUS APPLICATION

Whether called a "financial affidavit," "financial declaration," or an "income and expense declaration," representations made by a party on these pleadings often are the primary basis in the court's determination of a child support award. Misrepresentation on these pleadings is rampant. Gone unchecked and/or without requests for supporting documentation, abuse can and likely will occur.

Additionally, many parties request the courts to waive the filing fees because of their reported inability to pay. These financial affidavits, often called "In Forma Pauperus" Applications are sworn representations of the applying party's income and expenses. Once the form is filed it is often forgotten. A sharp opponent will compare the representations made on this initial affidavit with the sworn representations made at the time of the child support hearing. On occasion you will discover grave inconsistencies that will aid in the impeachment of your spouse's credibility.

DEVIATIONS FROM CHILD SUPPORT GUIDELINES

The court may allow a deviation for the child support guidelines if the court finds that there are special needs of the child or extraordinary earnings of the parent. Generally, it is purely at the discretion of your judge as to whether he will permit a deviation from the guidelines.

Examples of grounds for deviation from the guidelines that might translate into a greater child support award are as follows:

- The domiciliary parent's use of the family home in lieu of partial payment of support
- The extraordinary medical expenses relating to the child, not covered by insurance
- The special educational needs and related expenses of the child
- The extraordinary expenses of the child
- The extraordinary length of time that a child spends with the parent receiving child support

Examples of grounds for deviation from the guidelines that might translate into a smaller child support award are as follows:

- The income of a parent far exceeds the financial needs of a child
- The medical limitations and disabilities of a parent
- The wages earned and received by a child

- The extraordinary length of time that a child spends with the parent paying child support

The Federal Office of Child Support Enforcement compiled a list of the most common reasons that deviations from the guidelines were allowed.

Throughout America, reasons for deviation in child support awards are as follows:

- Agreement between the parents (21%)
- Needs of second households (14%)
- Extended or extraordinary visitation/custody expenses (13%)
- Non-custodial parent's low income (11%)
- An otherwise unjust result
- Extraordinary needs of the parent

Other common excuses heard in courts throughout the country for parents seeking to pay less child support include the following:

- Payer's physical or mental disabilities
- Payer's irregular or cyclical employment
- Custodial parent's interference with visitation rights
- Child support payments not benefiting children
- Payer paid for other items for children
- Not biological children
- Child is working
- Payer's incarceration

WATCH OUT FOR CANCELLATION OF INSURANCE POLICIES

Occasionally, upon the filing of a divorce action, a spouse may cancel the health, life and/or homeowner's insurance that covers you, your children, and your property. Ask your lawyer to file an "Ex Parte" motion for a temporary restraining order/injunction prohibiting these actions.

If your spouse cancels the insurance, your attorney should ask the court to compel him to re-instate the insurance and pay for any expenses that were incurred that would have been covered by the insurance had you or your child had been covered under the policy. Once again, ask your lawyer to file a motion for a temporary restraining order/injunction prohibiting the use of the policy.

WATCH OUT FOR 50-50 SPLIT OF OTHER CHILD RELATED EXPENSES

Lawyers and judges often suggest a 50-50 split of medical insurance, extraordinary medical expenses, day-care expenses, tuition, and the like. Whether such a proposal benefits you depends on what percentage of the two parents' combined gross income belongs to you.

DEPENDENCY TAX CREDIT

Ask for the Dependency Tax Credit.

TEMPORARY AWARD OF CHILD SUPPORT SETS THE TONE FOR REGULAR CHILD SUPPORT

A temporary award of child support and related child care expenses often later becomes a permanent award. A child support award is rarely reduced from the original temporary award. "Temporary" should not be equated to "not important" or "temporary" at all!

MODIFICATION OF CHILD SUPPORT

As long as the court maintains jurisdiction of the case and the child is eligible to receive the benefits of child support, the judge has the discretion to modify the child support award.

At the request of either party, the court can review the propriety of the child support award in effect. A party may seek a change in child support based on a "substantial" and/or "material" change of circumstance (either increase or decrease) in a party's income, financial needs of the child, when one child becomes ineligible by age or other factors such as emancipation, or where medical support has not been considered.

Many states have no criteria to determine what dollar change is required to be considered "substantial." Other states have provided standards to provide pecuniary measures as to whether a change is "substantial." Some states require a change in a party's average gross income, while others look to the proposed change in the actual child support award. "Substantial" could be defined as, as little as $50.00 or a ten (10%) percent change or as much of a minimum requirement of $100.00 or a thirty (30%) percent change. In many cases, the criteria established to allow a modification in child support are not rigidly followed.

As a recipient or payer of child support who has not sought a review in the award within the last several years, you should inquire as to whether an increase or decrease is in order. Your attorney's request for various income and expense documents may assist you in this evaluation. Child support cases that involve AFDC, Title IV-E Foster Care and/or Non-AFDC Medicaid should be reviewed every three years.

WHEN PAYMENTS OF CHILD SUPPORT SHOULD BE MADE

Although a moral obligation to pay child support begins at the child's birth, in most states, a legal obligation to pay child support does not begin until it is requested by filing a pleading in court. In some states, the child support obligation is only retroactive to the date of filing for child support. Hence, it is important for the custodial parent to file for child support as soon as possible after the child is born.

Once a legal obligation of child support is created by law and/or by a judgment of a court, then the timing of the payments must be established. Courts often require payments each month, each week, every two weeks, or on the payer's paycheck cycle.

A payer of child support may not get credit for payments made to the custodial parent that were made prior to the custodial parent's formal request to the court for the support. Likewise, a payer of child support may not get credit against his child support obligation for the payment of child-related goods, such as diapers, food, and clothing.

Can the payer deduct for his expenses? Generally — no

For the payer to receive full credit for each cent that is paid in child support, the payments should be made directly to the recipient custodial parent.

GET PROOF OF PAYMENT

A payer should be able to prove payment of child support for a specified time period (i.e., month) by specifying in the memo of the check the following:

1. Payment of "Child Support"
2. Date (include period covered — i.e., "December of 2014")

> Example:
> *"Memo: Child Support for January of 2015"*

The burden of proof that a child support payment was made generally falls on the payer. Regardless of whether you are the recipient or payer of child support, you should keep records and copies of all child support payments. This shall assist you if a dispute occurs at a later date.

Best Methods of Payment:

1. Pay by personal check (Keep canceled checks and check registry)
   The payer should keep photocopies of checks in case the bank does not return canceled checks.
2. Pay by money orders or cashier's checks (keep copies)
3. Mail by "Certified Mail, Return Receipt Requested"
4. Pay through the child support enforcement agency or clerk of the court
5. Pay through an income assignment

A PAYER SHOULD NEVER PAY IN CASH

Cash is the worst method of payment of child support. Unless a receipt is made and signed by both parties, proof becomes a swearing match. Furthermore, receipts may become suspect in cases where a spouse has threatened violence unless the custodial parent signed a fake receipt.

Payment should be made on or before the due date. Make sure that the payment is received by the recipient on or before the date ordered. If the payment is due on the first of each month, then it should be mailed before and not on the first day of the month.

Be careful of setting a precedent in child support. Many people who pay child support make the personal mistake of paying child support to the recipient parent in an amount much greater than the amount reasonably expected to be ordered to pay at the child support hearing. Many times, these "excessive" payments are made out of guilt or other emotions. The payer should realize that the continual excessive payment of child support could set a precedent which the court feels is appropriate at the time of the hearing.

A more safe and accurate approach to paying the appropriate amount of child support is with the help of your lawyer. Your attorney can use your state's guidelines and suggest a figure that is fair.

It should be noted that any parent who has the ability and the desire to pay more child support than would be ordered should be commended.

Many parents who are ordered to pay child support complain that the other parent is not spending the child support money on the children. Most courts will not entertain discussions in this area unless the payer can prove that the custodial parent is neglecting to pay for the necessities of the children.

BANKRUPTCY AND CHILD SUPPORT

The payer of child support cannot interrupt his legal obligation to pay child support by filing bankruptcy. Furthermore, past-due child support is not dischargeable in bankruptcy.

A payer of child support may be subject to many court sanctions if he is continually late in his payment of child support. The penalties and sanctions are listed below.

RETROACTIVITY OF CHILD SUPPORT JUDGMENT

It is important for your attorney to file his or her pleadings requesting child support as soon as practicable as Louisiana courts usually will grant a custodial parent with retroactive child support from the date of filing of the pleading requesting child support. It is also important that one remind the payor spouse that he or she may be responsible for the payment of the child support retroactively so that the prospective payor can start making payments in which he or she will receive credit if the payments are made subsequent to the filing.

LA-R.S. 9:315.21 Retroactivity of child support judgment

A. Except for good cause shown, a judgment awarding, modifying, or revoking an interim child support allowance shall be retroactive to the date of judicial demand, but in no case prior to the date of judicial demand.

B. (1) A judgment that initially awards or denies final child support is effective as of the date the judgment is signed and terminates an interim child support allowance as of that date.

(2) If an interim child support allowance award is not in effect on the date of the judgment awarding final child support, the judgment shall be retroactive to the date of judicial demand, except for good cause shown, but in no case prior to the date of judicial demand.

C. Except for good cause shown, a judgment modifying or revoking a final child support judgment shall be retroactive to the date of judicial demand, but in no case prior to the date of judicial demand.

D. Child support of any kind, except that paid pursuant to an interim child support allowance award, provided by the judgment debtor from the date of judicial demand to the date the support judgment is signed, to or on behalf of the child for whom support is ordered, shall be credited to the judgment debtor against the amount of the judgment.

E. In the event that the court finds good cause for not making the award retroactive to the date of judicial demand, the court may fix the date on which the award shall commence, but in no case shall this date be a date prior to the date of judicial demand.

WHEN CHILD SUPPORT ENDS

Child support usually ends when a child reaches the "age of majority." Society deems the age of majority as the point in a child's life when he is able to be legally independent from his parents. To be declared legally and financially independent is referred to as being "emancipated." Emancipation is an event that generally terminates a child support obligation.

The "age of majority" of a child, in reference to the termination of child support, varies from state to state. The following states generally terminate child support upon the child reaching the age of 18:

Alaska, Arkansas, Arizona, Connecticut, Delaware, Florida, Georgia, Idaho, Iowa, Kansas, Kentucky, <u>Louisiana</u>, Massachusetts, Maine, Maryland, Michigan, Minnesota, Missouri, Nevada, New Mexico, North Carolina, North Dakota, Ohio, Oklahoma, Oregon, Pennsylvania, Rhode Island, South Carolina, South Dakota, Tennessee, Texas, Utah, Vermont, Virgin Islands, Virginia, Washington, West Virginia, Wisconsin, and Wyoming.

Of the above referenced states, most states, including Louisiana, have provisions for the continuation of child support beyond a specified age based on extraordinary medical or educational circumstances (generally until the age of 19).

States such as Hawaii and Massachusetts allow the extension of the obligation of child support through to the age of 23, if the child is enrolled in full-time higher education.

Washington D.C., Mississippi, New York, and Puerto Rico consider the age of majority as being 21.

As there are currently no uniform laws as to the definition of the "age of majority" throughout the United States, theoretically a custodial parent with a child could move from one state that defines the "age of majority" as 18 to a state that has an "age of majority" as 21, and extend the child support obligation for another three years.

Events that may create a basis to terminate child support throughout the nation are the following:
1. Obtaining the "age of majority"
2. Marriage of the child

3. Death of the child
4. Completion of the child's education
5. The child entering the military
6. The child's full-time employment and
7. The incarceration of the child (going to jail)

BASIS FOR EXTENDING CHILD SUPPORT OBLIGATION BEYOND THE "AGE OF MAJORITY"

There are two basic reasons that a child support obligation could extend beyond the child reaching his "age of majority":
1. The child has serious medical problems
2. The child remains in secondary school

Each state has laws that control one's eligibility to extend child support payments beyond the child's "age of majority." One thought is extremely prudent:

If a parent wants an extension of child support payments beyond the "age of majority," then the parent should formally seek an extension from the court prior to the child reaching that age. When one or more children reach the "age of majority," the entire child support obligation may be affected.

When parents have two or more minor children, a critical question arises as to what happens to the child support obligation when one of the children reaches the age of majority (or the child support obligation related to that child otherwise ends).

One of two circumstances can occur:

1.   The amount of the child support obligation continues unchanged

2.   The amount of the child support obligation is reduced

Prior to any of your children reaching the age of majority, consult your attorney and see how that event will affect you. A child support agreement or order can have provisions for a change in the child support award upon the occurrence of certain events (i.e., a child reaching the "age of majority"). Furthermore, a child support award can be calculated in increments based on a "per child" basis.

File for modifications, termination, or extension in child support in advance of event. Although a change or termination in a child support obligation may be automatic by the occurrence of an event such as the child's attainment of the "age of majority," it is inadvisable to assume that a modification, termination or extension in the obligation occurs without a formal request to the court. Speak with your lawyer to determine whether an action with the court is required. Failure to check with your lawyer, prior to the event, could be a costly mistake.

LA-R.S. 9:315.22 Termination of child support upon majority or emancipation; exceptions

A. When there is a child support award in a specific amount per child, the award for each child shall terminate automatically without any action by the obligor upon each child's attaining the age of majority, or upon emancipation relieving the child of the disabilities attached to minority.

B. When there is a child support award in globo for two or more children, the award shall terminate automatically and without any action by the obligor when the youngest child for whose benefit the award was made attains the age of majority or is emancipated relieving the child of the disabilities attached to minority.

C. An award of child support continues with respect to any unmarried child who attains the age of majority, or to a child who is emancipated relieving the child of the disabilities attached to minority, as long as the child is a full- time student in good standing in a secondary school or its equivalent, has not attained the age of nineteen, and is dependent upon either parent. Either the primary domiciliary parent or the major or emancipated child is the proper party to enforce an award of child support pursuant to this Subsection.

D. An award of child support continues with respect to any child who has a developmental disability, as defined in R.S. 28:381, until he attains the age of twenty-two, as long as the child is a full-time student in a secondary school. The primary domiciliary parent or legal guardian is the proper party to enforce an award of child support pursuant to this Subsection.

INCOME ASSIGMENT/GARNISHMENT

Louisiana courts should order that the child support obligation is paid through an income assignment or garnishment unless agreed in writing by the parties. The parties may wish to make other payment arrangements as the government body that administers that income assignment usually charges the payor an additional fee which generally ranges from 3 to 5% of the monthly child support obligation.

LA-R.S. 9:303 Income assignment; new orders; deviation

A. In all new child support orders after January 1, 1994, that are not being enforced by the Department of Social Services, the court shall include as part of the order an immediate income assignment unless there is a written agreement between the parties or the court finds good cause not to require an immediate income assignment.

B. For purposes of this Section:

(1) "Written agreement" means a written alternative arrangement signed by both parents, reviewed by the court, and entered into the record of the proceedings.

(2) "Good cause" exists upon a showing by the respondent that any of the following exist:

(a) There has been no delinquency in payment of child support for the six calendar months immediately preceding the filing of the motion for modification of an existing child support order.

(b) The respondent is agreeable to a consent judgment authorizing an automatic ex parte immediate income assignment if he becomes delinquent in child support payments for a period in excess of one calendar month.

(c) The respondent is not likely to become delinquent in the future.

(d) Any other sufficient evidence which, in the court's discretion, constitutes good cause.

C. An income assignment order issued pursuant to this Section shall be payable through the Louisiana state disbursement unit for collection and disbursement of child support payments as provided in R.S. 46:236.11 and shall be governed by the same provisions as immediate income assignment orders that are being enforced by the department, including R.S. 46:236.3 and 236.4. All clerks of court in the state shall provide information to the state disbursement unit on income assignment orders issued pursuant to this Section. The department shall promulgate rules and regulations to implement the provisions of this Section in accordance with the Administrative Procedure Act.

REDUCTION OR INCREASE IN CHILD SUPPORT

In order to receive a change from a prior support judgment, the party seeking the change must prove a material change in circumstances as set forth in LA-R.S. 9:311.

LA-R.S. 9:311 Reduction or increase in support; material change in circumstances; periodic review by DSS; medical support

A. An award for support shall not be reduced or increased unless the party seeking the reduction or increase shows a material change in circumstances of one of the parties between the time of the previous award and the time of the motion for modification of the award.

B. A judgment for past due support shall not of itself constitute a material change in circumstances of the obligor sufficient to reduce an existing award of support.

C. For purposes of this Section, in cases where the Department of Social Services is providing support enforcement services:

(1) A material change in circumstance exists when a strict application of the child support guidelines, Part I-A of this Chapter, would result in at least a twenty-five percent change in the existing child support award. A material change in circumstance does not exist under this Paragraph if the amount of the award was the result of the court's deviating from the guidelines pursuant to R.S. 9:315.1 and there has not been a material change in the circumstances which warranted the deviation.

(2) Upon request of either party or on its own initiative and if the best interest of the child so requires, the department shall provide for judicial

review and, if appropriate, the court may adjust the amount of the existing child support award every three years if the existing award differs from the amount which would otherwise be awarded under the application of the child support guidelines. The review provided hereby does not require a showing of a material change in circumstance nor preclude a party from seeking a reduction or increase under the other provisions of this Section.

D. A material change in circumstance need not be shown for purposes of modifying a child support award to include a court-ordered award for medical support.

E. If the court does not find good cause sufficient to justify an order to modify child support or the motion is dismissed prior to a hearing, it may order the mover to pay all court costs and reasonable attorney fees of the other party if the court determines the motion was frivolous.

F. The provisions of Subsection E of this Section shall not apply when the recipient of the support payments is a public entity acting on behalf of another party to whom support is due.

ACCOUNTING OF CHILD SUPPORT

LA-R.S. 9:312 Child support; accounting; requirements

A. On motion of the party ordered to make child support payments pursuant to court decree, by consent or otherwise, after a contradictory hearing and a showing of good cause based upon the expenditure of child support for the six months immediately prior to the filing of the motion, the court shall order the recipient of the support payments to render an accounting.

B. The accounting ordered by the court after the hearing shall be in the form of an expense and income affidavit for the child with supporting documentation and shall be provided quarterly to the moving party. The order requiring accounting in accordance with this Section shall continue in effect as long as support payments are made or in accordance with the court order.

C. The movant shall pay all court costs and attorney fees of the recipient of child support when the motion is dismissed prior to the hearing, and the court determines the motion was frivolous, or when, after the contradictory hearing, the court does not find good cause sufficient to justify an order requiring the recipient to render such accounting and the court determines the motion was frivolous.

D. The provisions of this Section shall not apply when the recipient of the support payments is a public entity acting on behalf of another party to whom support is due.

DON'T RESTRICT VISITATION BECAUSE OF A REFUSAL TO PAY CHILD SUPPORT

It is commonly tempting to refuse or restrict visitation if the payer is not providing child support payments as ordered. Unless a refusal or restriction of visitation is pursuant a "linkage order" (discussed later in this chapter), then the custodial parent is exposing himself to contempt of court sanctions. Also remember that the custodial parent must be a "good parent" for the child's sake. Let the judge do his job, and deal with the non-paying parent. Let the wrath of the court come down only on the delinquent payer; otherwise, the wrath of the court may come down on both of you.

Another unintended result might occur. A few courts have ordered that child support payments are suspended where a custodial parent has intentionally refused and/or interfered with visitation rights.

Always remember that the child suffers by a refusal or restriction of visitation rights (unless the visiting parent is neglectful or abusive). The payment of child support and visitation generally are separate issues.

Non-custodial parents who have joint custody and/or visitation rights are more likely to pay child support than those parents that do not have these rights. Of the 11.5 million non-custodial parents, 6.9 million have joint custody of their children. (U.S. Census Bureau)

THE UNIFORM RECIPROCAL ENFORCEMENT OF SUPPORT ACT (URESA)

This federal act was created in 1950 to assist in the uniform enforcement of child support orders across state lines. In 1968, the act was revised. States' use of URESA is decreasing as it has only marginal desirability and effectiveness. Under URESA, a person seeking child support would request the attorney to file a petition in their "initiating" state. The pleadings would be sent to the "responding" state where the noncustodial parent lives or owns property. It was the responsibility of the foreign responding state to establish and/or enforce a child support order. Under URESA, a noncustodial parent could argue before his or her home state ("responding state") that a reduction in the amount is sought. The possibility of more than one child support order could exist under URESA, thus creating a child support discrepancy between the "initiating" and "responding" state's orders.

Many states have repealed their URESA legislation in favor of the Uniform Interstate Family Support Act (UIFSA).

THE UNIFORM INTERSTATE FAMILY SUPPORT ACT (UIFSA)

Under UIFSA, the establishment and enforcement of a child support obligation is assisted with one order. Unless agreed by both parents, UIFSA provides that the state that originally makes the child support decree continues to have jurisdiction ("continuing exclusive jurisdiction") as long as one parent continues to reside in the state. This insures that only one child support order is in effect. Courts evaluate whether jurisdiction exists on a case by case basis. The court will consider the following factors in deciding whether jurisdiction exists:

1.   Whether the noncustodial parent is personally served in the state
2.   Whether the noncustodial parent consents to the jurisdiction of the state
3.   Whether the noncustodial parent had resided with the child within the state
4.   Whether the noncustodial parent had sexual intercourse in the state that lead to the conception of the child
5.   Whether the child resides in the state as a result of any action of the noncustodial parent
6.   Whether the noncustodial parent acknowledged the child in the state and/or
7.   Any other facts that the court deems relevant

UIFSA legislation allows one state's income withholding order to be directly sent to an employer of the noncustodial parent in another UIFSA state.

Each state has a Central Registry for the collection of interstate child support orders. A listing of each state's Central Registry is found in the Appendix.

Your lawyer can give you more information on how these federal acts affect one's ability to collect child support.

REPORT PROBLEMS TO THE OFFICE OF CHILD SUPPORT ENFORCEMENT

If you find that a certain agency or court is failing to pursue the enforcement of your order awarding child support, you may seek assistance by reporting the problems, via certified mail, to the following federal office:

Federal Parent Locator Service
Department of Health and Human Services
Family Support Administration
Office of Child Support Enforcement
4th Floor
370 L'Enfant Promenade S.W.
Washington D.C. 20447
(202) 252-5443 (Federal Parent Locator Service)
(202) 252-5343 (Family Support Administration)
(202) 475-0257 (Department of Health and Human Resources)

The Office of Child Support Enforcement (OCSE) is an agency of the United Stated Department of Health and Human Services which works in conjunction with state agencies. The OCSE assists in locating missing parents, establishing paternity, and establishing and collecting collect support. The OCSE also may assist in the collection of alimony if the past due alimony is due pursuant to a prior order establishing both alimony and child support.

The OCSE will not assist a party in obtaining a divorce, property settlement, and/or the pursuit of a new order for alimony.
Quick Facts

In a recent year, state child support enforcement agencies established over a million new child support orders, enforced and/or modified over five million child support orders, and collected $10.8 billion dollars in child support payments. In the same period, the state agencies also established paternity for 903,400 children.

State Child Support Offices assist in the following:
1.   Locating non-custodial parents
2.   Establishing paternity
3.   Establishing child support orders and/or
4.   Enforcing child support orders/collecting child support

Louisiana's Office of Support Enforcement Services is as follows:

Louisiana Enforcement Services
Department of Health and Human Services
P.O. Box 44276
Baton Rouge, LA 70804
(504) 342-4780
http://www.dss.state.la.us/mainfram.htm

LOUISIANA DEPARTMENT OF SOCIAL SERVICES CHILD SUPPORT ENFORCEMENT SERVICES REGIONAL OFFICES

Alexandria
900 Murray Street
P.O. Box 832
Alexandria, LA 71309-0832
(318) 487-5202
Covered Parishes: Avoyelles, Catahoula, Concordia, Grant, LaSalle, Rapides, Vernon, and Winn

Amite
407 N.W. Central Avenue
P. O. Box 338
Amite, LA 70422-0338
(504) 748-2006
Covered Parishes: Livingston, St. Helena, St. Tammany, Tangipahoa, and Washington

Baton Rouge
333 Laurel Street, Second Floor
P.O. Box 829
Baton Rouge, LA 70821
(225) 342-5760

Covered Parishes: Ascension, Assumption, East
Baton Rouge, East Feliciana, Iberville, Pointe
Coupee, St. James, West Baton Rouge, and West
Feliciana

Gretna
802 Second Street
Gretna, LA 70053
Covered Parish: Jefferson

Lafayette
825 Kaliste Saloom Road, Suite 200
P. O. Box 3867
Lafayette, LA 70508-3867
(337) 262-5813
Covered Parishes: Acadia, Iberia, Lafayette,
St.Martin, St. Mary, and Vermilion

Lake Charles
1417 Gadwell Street
Lake Charles, LA 70615
(337) 491-2111
Covered Parishes: Beauregard, Calcasieu, Cameron,
and Jefferson Davis

Monroe
2006 Tower Drive
P. O. Box 3144
Monroe, LA 71210-3144
(318) 362-5271
Covered Parishes: Bienville, Caldwell, Claiborne,
Franklin, Jackson, Lincoln, Morehouse, Ouachita,
Richland, Union, and West Monroe

Natchitoches
1774 Texas Street

P. O. Box 1317
Natchitoches, LA 71458
(318) 357-3109
Covered Parishes: DeSoto, Natchitoches, Red River, and Sabine

New Orleans
2235 Poydras Street
P. O. Box 53446
New Orleans, LA 70153-3446
(504) 826-2222
Covered Parishes: Orleans, Plaquemines, and St. Bernard

Shreveport
9310 Normandie Drive
P. O. Box 18590
Shreveport, LA 71138
(318) 676-7010
Covered Parishes: Bossier, Caddo, and Webster

Tallulah
1614 Felicia Drive
P. O. Box 431
Tallulah, LA 71282-0431
(318) 574-0486
Covered Parishes: East Carroll, Madison, and Tensas

Thibodaux
1000-A Plantation Road
P. O. Box 1427
Thibodaux, LA 70302-1427
(985) 447-0952
Covered Parishes: Lafouche, St. Charles, St. John, and Terrebonne

Ville Platte
318 Nita Drive
P. O. Box 119
Ville Platte, LA 70586
(337) 363-6638
Covered Parishes: Allen, Evangeline, and St. Landry

STATE CHILD SUPPORT ENFORCEMENT OFFICES IN AMERICA

Alabama
Division of child Support Activities
Bureau of Public Assistance
State Department of Pensions and Security
64 N. Union Street
Montgomery, AL 36130
(205) 242-9300
http://www.state.al.us/

Alaska
Child Support Enforcement Agency
Department of Revenue
201 E. 9th Avenue, Room 302
Anchorage, AK 99501
(907) 276-3441
http://www.revenue.state.ak.us/csed/csed.htm.

Arizona
Child Support Enforcement Administration
Department of Economic Security
P.O. Box 6123, Site Code 966C
Phoenix, AZ 85005
(602) 255-3465
http://aztec.asu.edu/cirs/alpha/1360.html

Arkansas
Office of Child Support Enforcement
Arkansas Social Services
P.O. Box 3358
Little Rock, AR 72203
(501) 371-2464
http://www.state.ar.us/

California
Child Support, Program Management Branch
Department of Social Services
744 P Street
Sacramento, CA 95814
(916) 323-8994
http://www.childsup.cahwnet.gov.

Colorado
Division of Child Support Enforcement
Department of Social Services
1575 Sherman Street, Room 423
Denver, CO 80203
(303) 866-2442
http://www.dss.state.ct.us/svcs/csupp.htm

Connecticut
Bureau of Child Support
1049 Asylum Avenue Resources
Hartford, CT 06105
(203) 566-3053
(800) 228-KIDS (5437)
http://www.dss.state.ct.us/svcs/csupp.htm

Delaware
Services for Children, Youth and Their Families
Program Support Division
1825 Faulkland Road

Wilmington, DE 19805
(302) 633-2670
http://www.state.de.us

District of Columbia
Bureau of Child Support Enforcement
Department of Human Services
3rd Floor
425 I Street, NW
Washington, D.C. 20001
(202) 724-56610

Florida
Office of Child Support Enforcement
Department of Health and Rehabilitative Services
1317 Winewood Boulevard
Tallahassee, FL 32301
(904) 488-9900
http://fcn.state.fl.us/dor/cse.html

Georgia
Office of Child Support Enforcement
P.O. Box 80000
Atlanta, GA 30357
(404) 894-5087
http://www.state.ga.us/Departments/dhr/cse/

Guam
Child Support Enforcement Unit
Department of Public Health and Social Services
Government of Guam
P.O. Box 2816
Agana, GU 96910
(671) 734-2947

Hawaii
Child Support Enforcement Agency
770 Dapiolani Boulevard, Suite 606Honolulu, HI
96813
(808) 548-5779
http://www.hawaii.gov/csea/csea.htm

Idaho
Bureau of Child Support Enforcement
Department of Health and Welfare
Statehouse Mail
Boise, ID 83720
(208) 334-4422
http://www.state.id.us/

Illinois
Bureau of Child Support
Department of Public Aid
316 south Second Street
Springfield, IL 62762
(217) 782-1366
http://www.state.il.us/dpa/cse.htm

Indiana
Child Support Enforcement division
State Department of Public Welfare
4th Floor
141 South Merridian Street
Indianapolis, IN 46224
(317) 232-4894
http://www.ai.org/fssa/cse/

Iowa
Child Support Recovery Unit
Iowa Department of Social Services
1st Floor
Hoover Building

Des Moines, IA 50319
(515) 281-5580
http://www2.legis.state.ia.us/ga/76ga/legislation/sf/0
2300/sf02344/current.htl

Kansas
Child Support Enforcement Program
Department of Social and Rehabilitation Services
Perry Building, 1st Floor
2700 West Sixth
Topeka, KS 66606
(913) 296-3237
http://www.ink.org/public/srs/srswanted.html

Kentucky
Human Resources Cabinet
Family Services Division
275 East Main Street
Frankfort, KY 40621
(502) 564-6852
http://www.state.ky.us/oag/childs.htm

Louisiana
Louisiana Enforcement Services
Department of Health and Human Services
P.O. Box 44276
Baton Rouge, LA 70804
(504) 342-4780
http://www.dss.state.la.us/mainfram.htm

Maine
Support Enforcement and Location Unit
Department of Human Services
State House Station II
Augusta, ME 04333
(207) 289-2886
http://www.state.me.us/

Maryland
Child Support Enforcement Administration
Department of Human Resources
5th Floor
300 West Preston Street
Baltimore, MD 21201
(301) 383-4773
          http://www.state.md.us/srv_csea.htm

Massachusetts
Child Support Enforcement Unit
Massachusetts Department of Revenue
213 First Street
Cambridge, MA 02142
(617) 621-4759
http://www.mst,oa.net:8002/macse.html

Michigan
Office of Child Support Enforcement
Department of Social Services
P.O. Box 30037
Landsing, MI 48909
(517) 373-7570
http://www.mfia.state.mi.us

Minnesota
Department of Human Services
Space Center Building
444 Lafayette Road
St. Paul, MN 55101
(612) 296-2499
http://www.co.hennnepin.mnus/weapsupp.html

Mississippi
Child Support Division
State Department of Public Welfare
P.O. Box 352
515 East Amite Street
Jackson, MS 39205
(601) 354-0341
http://www.mdhs.state.ms.us/cse.html

Missouri
Child Support Enforcement Unit
Division of Family Services
Department of Social Services
P.O. Box 88
Jefferson City, MO 65103
(314) 751-4301
http://services.state.mo.us/dss/cse/cse.htm

Montana
Child Support Enforcement Bureau
P.O. Box 5955
Helena, MT 59604
(406) 444-3347
http://www.dphhs.mt.gov/whowhat/csed.htm

Nebraska
Office of Child Support Enforcement
Department of Social Services
P.O. Box 95026
Lincoln, NE 68509
(402) 471-3121
http://www.unl.edu/ccfl/cse.htm

Nevada
Child Support Enforcement Program
Welfare Division
2527 North Carson Street
Carson City, NV 89710
(702) 885-4474
http://state.mv.us/

New Hampshire
Office of Child Support Enforcement
Division of Welfare
Health and Welfare Building
Hazen Drive
Concord, NH 03301
(603) 271-4426
http://little.nhlink.net/nhlink/governme/county/dhs/
chld_sup.htm

New Jersey
Child Support and Paternity Unit
Department of Human Services
CN 716
Trenton, NJ 08625
(609) 633-6268
http://www.state.nj.us/judiciary/prob01.htm

New Mexico
Child Support Enforcement Bureau
Department of Human Services
P.O. Box 2348 –PERA Building
Santa Fe, NM 85793
(505) 827-4230
http://www.mostwanted.com/nh/support.htm

New York
Office of Child Support Enforcement
Albany, NY 12260
(518) 474-9081
http://www.state.ny.us/dss/

North Carolina
Child Support Enforcement Section
Division of Social Services
Department of Human Resources
433 North Harrington Street
Raleigh, NC 27603
(919) 733-4120
http://www.state.nc.us/cse/

North Dakota
Child Support Enforcement Agency
North Dakota Department of Human Services
State Capitol
Bismark, ND 58505
(701) 224-3582
http://www.state.nd.us/hms/

Ohio
Bureau of Child Support
Ohio Department of Human Services
State Office Tower
31st Floor
30 East Broad Street
Columbus, OH 43215
(614) 466-3233
http://www.ohiogov/odhs/

Oklahoma
Division of Child Support
Department of Human Services
P.O. Box 25352
Oklahoma City, OK 73125
(405) 424-5871
http://www.acf.dhhs.gov/acfprograms/cse/fct/sp_ok.
html

Oregon
Child Support Program
Department of Human Resources
Adult and Family Services Division
P.O. Box 14506
Salem, OR 97309
(503) 378-6093
http://170.104.17.50/rss/rogues.html

Pennsylvania
Child Support Enforcement Program
Department of Public Welfare
P.O. Box 8018
Harrisburg, PA 17105
(717) 783-1779
http://www.state.pa.us/pa_exec/public_welfare/over
view.html

Puerto Rico
Child Support Enforcement
Department of Social Services
Ferninandez Juncos Station
P.O. Box 11398
Santurce, PR 00910
(809) 722-4731

Rhode Island
Bureau of Family Support
Department of Social and Rehabilitative Services
77 Dorance Street
Providence, RI 02903
(401) 277-2409
http://www.state.ri.us/

South Carolina
Division of Child Support
Public Assistance Division
Bureau of Public Assistance and Field Operations
Department of Social Services
P.O. Box 1520
Columbia, SC 29202
(803) 758-8860
http://www.state.sc.us/

South Dakota
Office of Child Support Enforcement
Department of Social Services
700 Illinois Street
Pierre, SD 57501
(605) 773-3641
http://www.state.sd.us/state/executive/social/social.h
tml

Tennessee
Child Support Services
Department of Human Services
5th floor
111-19 Seventh Avenue
Nashville, TN 37203
(615) 741-1820
http://www.state.tn.us/humanserv/

Texas
Child Support Enforcement Branch
Texas Department of Human Resources
P.O. Box 2960
Austin, TX 78769
(512) 463-2005
http://www.oag.state.tx.us/website/childsup.htm

Utah
Office of Recovery Services
P.O. Box 15400
3195 South Main Street
Salt Lake City, UT 84115
(801) 486-1812
http://www.state.ut.us/

Vermont
Child Support Division
Department of Social Welfare
103 South Main Street
Waterbury, VT 05676
(802) 241-2868
http://www.dsw.state.vt.us/ahs/ahs.htm

Virgin Islands
Paternity and Child Support Program
Department of Law
P.O. Box 1074
Christiansted
St. Croix, VI 00820
(809) 773-8240

Virginia
Division of Support Enforcement Program
Department of Social Services
8004 Franklin Farm Drive
Richmond, VA 23288
(804) 662-9108
http://www.state.va.us/-dss/childspt.html

Washington
Office of Child Support Enforcement
Department of Social and Health Services
P.O. Box 9162-MS PI-11
Olympia, WA 98504
(206) 459-6481
http://www.wa.gov/dshs/csrc.html

West Virginia
Office of Child Support Enforcement
Department of Human Services
1900 Washington Street, East
Charleston, WV 25305
(304) 348-3780
http://www.state.wv.us/

Wisconsin
Department of Health and Human Services
Division of Community Services
1 West Wilson Street
P.O. Box 7851
Madison, WI 53707
(608) 266-9909
http://dhss.state.wi.us/dhss/pubs/html/childsp.html

Wyoming
Child Support Enforcement Section
Division of Public Assistance and Social Services
State Department of Health and Social Services
Hathaway Building
Cheyenne, WY 82002
(307) 777-6083
http://www.dfsweb.state.wy.us/csehome/wybody1.h

tm

INFORMATION AND DOCUMENTS TO BRING TO YOUR OFFICE OF CHILD SUPPORT ENFORCEMENT

1. Name of noncustodial parent
2. Last known address of noncustodial parent
3. Child's birth certificate
4. Any child support order
5. Any divorce decree (if applicable)
6. Last known name and address of noncustodial parent's employer
7. Any other information regarding the whereabouts and/or income/assets of the noncustodial parent

LOCATE "DEADBEATS"

The **PARENT LOCATOR SERVICE** is one of the most effective methods to track down non-custodial parents who live in or out of your state. The computerized system locates parents by the use of driver's license numbers, security numbers, and other means of identification.

States differ in the extent of their ability to trace a person through their state agencies. States typically contact the following sources:
- Credit Bureau Contacts
- Department of Corrections
- Department of Human Services (Food Stamps and other programs)
- Department of Labor/Employment Security (Food Stamps and Unemployment Benefits)
- Department of Public Safety/Motor Vehicles/Transportation
- Department of Revenue/Taxation
- Department of Social Services
- Department of Vital Statistics (Birth Certificates)
- Department of Wildlife and Fisheries (Fish and Game Licenses)
- IV-A/Medicaid Database
- New Hire Reporting System
- Registrar of Voters/Department of Elections (Voter Registration)
- Secretary of State

SUSPENSION OR MODIFICATION OF CHILD SUPPORT OBLIGATION WHEN SECRETING A CHILD

LA-R.S. 9:315.23 Suspension or modification of child support obligation; secreting of child

If one joint custodial parent or his agent is intentionally secreting a child with the intent to preclude the other joint custodial parent from knowing the whereabouts of the child sufficiently to allow him to exercise his rights or duties as joint custodial parent, the latter may obtain from the court an order suspending or modifying his obligation under an order or judgment of child support. However, such circumstances shall not constitute a defense to an action for failure to pay court-ordered child support or an action to enforce past due child support.

AWARD OF ATTORNEY FEES

LA-R.S. 9:375 Award of attorney's fees

A. When the court renders judgment in an action to make executory past-due payments under a spousal or child support award, or to make executory past-due installments under an award for contributions made by a spouse to the other spouse's education or training, it shall, except for good cause shown, award attorney's fees and costs to the prevailing party.

B. When the court renders judgment in an action to enforce child visitation rights it shall, except for good cause shown, award attorney's fees and costs to the prevailing party.

COSTS; ACTION TO MAKE CHILD SUPPORT EXECUTORY

LA-R.S. 9:304.1 Costs; action to make child support executory

A. An action to make past due child support executory may be filed by any plaintiff, who is unable to utilize the provisions of Chapter 5 of Title I of Book IX of the Code of Civil Procedure, without paying the costs of court in advance or as they accrue or furnishing security therefore, if the court is satisfied that the plaintiff because of poverty or lack of means cannot afford to make payment.

B. When the action has been filed without the payment of costs as provided in Subsection A and the plaintiff is not the prevailing party, except for good cause, the court shall order the plaintiff to pay all costs of court.

DISAVOWAL OF PATERNITY RELATING TO CHILD SUPPORT OBLIGATION

LA-R.S. 9:305 Disavowal of paternity; ancillary to child support proceeding

A. Notwithstanding the provisions of Civil Code Art. 189 and for the sole purpose of determining the proper payor in child support cases, if the husband, or legal father who is presumed to be the father of the child, erroneously believed, because of misrepresentation, fraud, or deception by the mother, that he was the father of the child, then the time for filing suit for disavowal of paternity shall be suspended during the period of such erroneous belief or for ten years, whichever ends first.

B. No provision of this Section shall affect any child support payment or arrears paid, due, or owing prior to the filing of a disavowal action if an order of disavowal is subsequently obtained in such action

SEMINAR FOR DIVORCING PARENTS

Louisiana courts often require the divorcing spouses to go to parenting classes to insure that the couple understands their responsibilities, including the financial obligation of child rearing.

CONTEMPT OF COURT

LA-R.S. 13:4611 Punishment for contempt of court
Except as otherwise provided for by law:

(1) The supreme court, the courts of appeal, the district courts, family courts, juvenile courts, and the city courts may punish a person adjudged guilty of a contempt of court therein, as follows:

(a) For a direct contempt of court committed by an attorney at law, by a fine of not more than one hundred dollars, or by imprisonment for not more than twenty-four hours, or both; and, for any subsequent contempt of the same court by the same offender, by a fine of not more than two hundred dollars, or by imprisonment for not more than ten days, or both;

(b) For disobeying or resisting a lawful restraining order, or preliminary or permanent injunction, by a fine of not more than one thousand dollars, or by imprisonment for not more than twelve months, or both, except in juvenile courts and city courts, in which punishment may be a fine of not more than one thousand dollars or imprisonment for not more than six months, or both.

(c) For a deliberate refusal to perform an act which is yet within the power of the offender to perform, by imprisonment until he performs the act; and

(d) For any other contempt of court, including disobeying an order for the payment of child support or spousal support or an order for the right of custody or visitation, by a fine of not more than five hundred dollars, or imprisonment for not more than three months, or both.

(e) In addition to or in lieu of the above penalties, when a parent has violated a visitation order, the court may order any or all of the following:

(i) Require one or both parents to allow additional visitation days to replace those denied the noncustodial parent.

(ii) Require one or both parents to attend a parent education course.

(iii) Require one or both parents to attend counseling or mediation.

(2) Justices of the peace may punish a person adjudged guilty of a direct contempt of court by a fine of not more than fifty dollars, or imprisonment in the parish jail for not more than twenty-four hours, or both.

(3) The court or justice of the peace, when applicable, may suspend the imposition or the execution of the whole or any part of the sentence imposed and place the defendant on unsupervised probation or probation supervised by a probation office, agency, or officer designated by the court or justice of the peace, other than the division of

probation and parole of the Department of Public Safety and Corrections. When the court or justice of the peace places a defendant on probation, the court or the justice of the peace may impose any specific conditions reasonably related to the defendant's rehabilitation, including but not limited to the conditions of probation as set forth in Code of Criminal Procedure Article 895. A term of probation shall not exceed the length of time a defendant may be imprisoned for the contempt, except in the case of contempt for disobeying an order for the payment of child support or spousal support or an order for the right of custody or visitation, when the term of probation may extend for a period of up to two years.

SUSPENSION OF LICENSES FOR NONPAYMENT OF CHILD SUPPORT

LA-R.S. 9:315.30 Family financial responsibility; purpose

The legislature finds and declares that child support is a basic legal right of the state's parents and children, that mothers and fathers have a legal obligation to provide financial support for their children, and that child support payments can have a substantial impact on child poverty and state welfare expenditures. It is therefore the legislature's intent to facilitate the establishment of paternity and child support orders and encourage payment of child support to decrease overall costs to the state's taxpayers while increasing the amount of financial support collected for the state's children. To this end, the courts of this state are authorized to suspend certain licenses of individuals who are found to be in contempt of court for failure to comply with a subpoena or warrant in a child support or paternity proceeding or who are not in compliance with a court order of child support.

RE-ISSUANCE OF LICENSE AFTER PAYMENT OF CHILD SUPPORT

LA-R.S. 9:315.35 Re-issuance of license

A. A board shall issue, reissue, renew, or otherwise extend an obligor's or other individual's license in accordance with the board's rules upon receipt of a certified copy of an order of compliance from the court.

B. After receipt of an order of compliance, the board may waive any of its applicable requirements for issuance, reissuance, renewal, or extension if it determines that the imposition of that requirement places an undue burden on the person and that waiver of the requirement is consistent with the public interest.

CRIMINAL NEGLECT OF FAMILY

LA-R.S. 14:74 Criminal neglect of family
A. (1) Criminal neglect of family is the desertion or intentional nonsupport:

(a) By a spouse of his or her spouse who is in destitute or necessitous circumstances; or

(b) By either parent of his minor child who is in necessitous circumstances, there being a duty established by this Section for either parent to support his child.

(2) Each parent shall have this duty without regard to the reasons and irrespective of the causes of his living separate from the other parent. The duty established by this Section shall apply retrospectively to all children born prior to the effective date of this Section.

(3) For purposes of this Subsection, the factors considered in determining whether "necessitous circumstances" exist are food, shelter, clothing, health, and with regard to minor children only, adequate education, including but not limited to public, private, or home schooling, and comfort.

B. (1) Whenever a husband has left his wife or a wife has left her husband in destitute or necessitous circumstances and has not provided means of support within thirty days thereafter, his or her failure to so provide shall be only presumptive evidence for the purpose of determining the substantive elements of this offense that at the time of leaving he or she intended desertion and nonsupport. The receipt of assistance from the Family Independence Temporary Assistance Program (FITAP) shall constitute only presumptive evidence of necessitous circumstances for purposes of proving the substantive elements of this offense. Physical incapacity which prevents a person from seeking any type of employment constitutes a defense to the charge of criminal neglect of family.

(2) Whenever a parent has left his minor child in necessitous circumstances and has not provided means of support within thirty days thereafter, his failure to so provide shall be only presumptive evidence for the purpose of determining the substantive elements of this offense that at the time of leaving the parent intended desertion and nonsupport. The receipt of assistance from the Family Independence Temporary Assistance Program (FITAP) shall constitute only presumptive evidence of necessitous circumstances for the purpose of proving the substantive elements of this offense. Physical incapacity which prevents a person from seeking any type of employment constitutes a defense to the charge of criminal neglect of family.

C. Laws attaching a privilege against the disclosure of communications between husband and wife are inapplicable to proceedings under this Section. Husband and wife are competent witnesses to testify to any relevant matter.

D. (1) Whoever commits the offense of criminal

neglect of family shall be fined not more than five hundred dollars or be imprisoned for not more than six months, or both, and may be placed on probation pursuant to R.S. 15:305.

(2) If a fine is imposed, the court shall direct it to be paid in whole or in part to the spouse or to the tutor or custodian of the child, to the court approved fiduciary of the spouse or child, or to the Louisiana Department of Social Services in a FITAP or Family Independence Temporary Assistance Program case or in a non-FITAP or Family Independence Temporary Assistance Program case in which the said department is rendering services, whichever is applicable; hereinafter, said payee shall be referred to as the "applicable payee." In addition, the court may issue a support order, after considering the circumstances and financial ability of the defendant, directing the defendant to pay a certain sum at such periods as the court may direct. This support shall be ordered payable to the applicable payee. The amount of support as set by the court may be increased or decreased by the court as the circumstances may require.

(3) The court may also require the defendant to enter into a recognizance, with or without surety, in order that the defendant shall make his or her personal appearance in court whenever required to do so and shall further comply with the terms of the order or of any subsequent modification thereof.

E. For the purposes of this Section, "spouse" shall mean a husband or wife.

LA-Ch.C. Art. 1353 CRIMINAL NEGLECT OF FAMILY; Support provisions; contempt; penalties

A. If the defendant violates the terms of the court order, the court, upon motion, may issue an order directing the defendant to show cause why he or she should not be found in contempt of court for failure to pay the court ordered support or maintain health care insurance, which rule shall be tried in a summary manner.

B. If on the hearing of such rule the court finds the accused guilty of contempt for failure to comply with the judgment of the court in paying the support assessed, the court may punish for such contempt as follows, either:

(1) The court may sentence the defendant to be imprisoned for not more than six months. The court in its discretion may suspend this term of imprisonment in whole or in part on condition that the defendant pay the total amount of unpaid support and obtain health care insurance in a manner to be determined by the court and on such other conditions as set by the court. If the court suspends the sentence in whole or in part, the court may place the defendant on probation under R.S. 15:305 with conditions of probation to be set by the court. In addition, the court may fine the defendant an amount not to exceed one hundred dollars to be paid to the applicable payee.

(2) The court may order the defendant to pay the total amount of unpaid support to the applicable payee and obtain health care insurance within a

period of time fixed by the court. During this period of time, the defendant may be released upon giving bond for his appearance in court if he fails to comply with the order of the court within the period of time fixed. Should the defendant not pay the total amount of unpaid support which the court has ordered, the defendant shall be imprisoned for not more than six months.

C. Upon a second or subsequent finding of contempt, the court shall sentence the defendant to imprisonment for not more than six months. At the discretion of the judge, the sentence may be suspended by the court upon the occurrence of all of the following:

(1) Payment of the amount of unpaid support.

(2) Payment of the amount of unpaid support accrued since the date of the said order.

(3) Payment of the amount of all attendant court costs.

(4) Proof of health care insurance.

D. Upon recommendation of the state attorney or the support enforcement officer, or both, the remainder of the sentence may be suspended upon payment of a lesser amount, plus attendant court costs. Such payment shall apply toward but not extinguish the total amount due.

E. If the court finds the accused guilty of contempt, the court shall also render judgment directing the defendant to obtain health care insurance and to pay the total amount of unpaid support to the applicable payee, and attendant court costs. Such judgment for the payment of unpaid support and court costs shall have the same force and effect as a final judgment for money damages against the defendant. This judgment may be made executory by any Louisiana court of competent jurisdiction on petition of the department or the district attorney.

F. If the defendant has entered into a recognizance in the amount fixed by the court to insure the payment of the support and maintenance of health care insurance, the court may order the forfeiture of the recognizance and enforcement thereof by execution. The sum recovered shall be paid in whole or in part to the applicable payee. However, should the court order both the forfeiture of the recognizance and at the same time order the defendant to pay all unpaid support under the sentence for contempt, the amount of unpaid support plus attendant court costs and fines shall be the maximum payable.

WATCH OUT FOR CHILD SUPPORT BLACKMAIL

It is all too common for a spouse to threaten a custody battle unless the other spouse concedes to a lower child support, alimony, and/or property settlement. This blackmail should not be tolerated. Report these threats to your attorney. Any evidence of these threats also should be given to your attorney.

STATUTE OF LIMITATIONS

A Statute of Limitations is the time period in which one can no longer seek enforcement of a former child support award. In many states, if a parent avoids payment of past due child support for a period of time longer than the state's statute of limitations, then that part of the child support obligation extending beyond the enforceable time period would be legally forgiven (exceptions do apply which your attorney can discuss with you in greater detail). For example, State "A" has a statute of limitations of five years. If the payer owes six years of back child support, then only the last five years of back child support would be legally collectible.

Some states have taken the enlightened view that a child support obligation is never excused by the mere passage of time.

Many states allow the child to pursue the past due child support after he or she reaches the age of majority.

CHAPTER 6

PREPARE FOR YOUR COURT DATE

YOUR SUCCESSFUL STEPS TO THIS POINT

Your trial date has arrived. With the help of this book, you are prepared because you have accomplished the following goals:

1. You have chosen the right attorney.
2. You made the appropriate fee arrangements with your attorney so that he had enough financial resources to do his job.
3. Your attorney has propounded discovery pleadings and appropriate responses have been given.
4. You have sufficiently tabled your emotions to be as persuasive as possible.
5. You have taken possession of your children, the house, the available money, other valuable documents, and other evidence.
6. Your lawyer has been successful in getting the judge to sign the appropriate restraining orders.
7. You have either attempted mediation or decided that it is not appropriate for your case.
8. You have weighed any settlement proposals that have been discussed between the parties.

9. In custody and visitation disputes, you have consciously weighed what is in the "best interests" of your children.
10.   You are ready to fight for your rights and the rights of your children.

If you have read this book in the middle of your domestic litigation, you may not have accomplished all of the goals set forth above. However, your chances of realistically achieving many of these goals is significantly enhanced by your application of the tips found in this book.

Knowing that you have become empowered through your preparation and knowledge, you should attempt to calm your concerns. Understand that it is natural to be nervous. Rest assured, your spouse should be nervous as well. Staying focused on your goals for the trial or hearing should channel the nervous energy into pure motivation to get the results that you want with your case.

BEFORE YOUR COURT DATE, GO AND WATCH YOUR JUDGE CONDUCT A TRIAL OR HEARING

As your trial approaches, pick a day to go to court when your judge is presiding over a domestic matter. This will give you a good idea of what you may expect on your trial date. Hopefully, this will alleviate some of your possible courtroom jitters. If you find that being a spectator in the courtroom has caused you more concerns, discuss your concerns with your attorney.   Remember, knowledge is power.

SEVERAL DAYS BEFORE TRIAL, SCHEDULE AN
OFFICE MEETING WITH YOUR ATTORNEY TO
GO OVER YOUR CASE AND TO ASK ANY
REMAINING QUESTIONS THAT YOU MAY
HAVE SETTLEMENT DISCUSSIONS

IT IS ALWAYS BETTER TO NEGOTIATE
FROM A POSITION OF STRENGTH
AND NOT WEAKNESS!

The information that you have gained and the preparation that you have made with your attorney should place you in a position of strength.

WHEN APPROPRIATE, ENTERTAIN
SETTLEMENT DISCUSSIONS

A judge does not like to hear that you have not had settlement discussions with your spouse. It may be advantageous for your attorney to tell the judge that you tried to resolve the matter and the other party would not cooperate. On the other hand, if there is no room for negotiations, any attempt to settle could be a sign of weakness and vulnerability. Discuss these thoughts with your attorney.

It may be possible for you to resolve some of the issues before the court. You are ready for trial after the settlement discussions have rendered only partial or no results.

ALL SETTLEMENT NEGOTIATIONS SHOULD BE HANDLED THROUGH YOUR ATTORNEY

By allowing your attorney to "relay" settlement proposals and responses to offers, you are lessening the chances for negotiations to break down because of the fragile emotional state of one or more of the parties.

ALWAYS NEGOTIATE LESS CONTROVERSIAL ISSUES FIRST

By negotiating less heated issues first, you are able to eliminate many issues that otherwise would be caught up in the emotional quagmire associated with other more volatile points of dispute (i.e., agree on who gets the use of which cars, and save the heated dispute on who gets custody of the children for last).

HAVE A PLAN AND KNOW YOUR "BOTTOM LINE"

It is wise to anticipate any settlement proposals that your spouse may make prior to going to trial. Many opponents strategically wait until trial begins to throw out a proposal that you would not remotely consider except while under the stress of the moment. By knowing your "bottom line," you can undermine these efforts and focus on the trail at hand. By preplanning a negotiation strategy, you have eliminated a potential plan of attack for a manipulative opponent.

Don't be swayed by emotions; and follow your intuition.

EVIDENCE USED AT TRIAL

Evidence can be elicited in three general ways:
1.   By stipulation
2.   By testimony
3.   By exhibits

Stipulations occur when both parties agree that:
1.   Certain "facts" be admitted into evidence as being true
2.   Certain "agreements of the parties" have been made that become a judgment of the court and/or

3.   Certain "documents and/or things" are admitted into evidence

WHO WILL TESTIFY?

Once the trial begins, witnesses will be called to testify under oath. Depending on the issues litigated, the witnesses called may include various people that have been discussed throughout the book.

"Lay" witnesses are witnesses who are not "experts" in a field that they are testifying in. They testify to facts as known through their own personal knowledge. These individuals could include persons such as the following:

Each parent, teachers, day-care providers, baby-sitters, nannies, coaches, doctors, dentists, priests, rabbis, neighbors, the children (if deemed mature enough), the children's friends (if deemed mature enough), boy scout leaders, girl scout leaders, school principals, Sunday school teachers, guidance counselors, police officers, housekeepers, private investigators, etc.

Usually, the court will limit the number of witnesses that are anticipated to testify in similar fashion.

"Expert" witnesses are persons that have an expertise recognized by the court. These persons are able to provide "expert opinions" based on information and/or hypothetical situations that are posed to them. Typically, expert witnesses include persons such as the following:

Psychiatrists, sociologists, other physicians, social workers, vocational rehabilitation experts, accountants, handwriting specialists, real estate appraisers, etc.

WHEN IT IS YOUR TURN TO TESTIFY

Here are some general tips to allow you to maximize your courtroom presentation:

Attire:
• Dress neatly (don't dress in "extremes" — either too causal or too formal)
• Do not wear a hat in court
• Do not chew gum
• Do not smoke
• Do not wear expensive jewelry
  Listen, wait, think, and then answer:
• Be truthful (you have not withheld information from your attorney)
• Be courteous and polite
• Listen to each question
• Pause and think of your answer before you respond to each question
• If you do not understand the question, tell the questioning attorney that   you do not understand the question and to restate or rephrase it
• If you do not know or recall the answer, say so

- Answer only the question asked
  Maintain self-control:
- Have good eye contact with the judge (and jury, if one exists)
- Do not swear or make obscene gestures
- Do not call your spouse bad names (i.e., "that despicable maggot in the   blue shirt")
- Do not speak to your spouse in the courtroom
- Do not let the opposing attorney get you angry and emotional
- Do not bring your children to court unless and until   you   have   a prior discussion with your attorney
- Be a gracious winner

> ## ALWAYS MAINTAIN GOOD EYE CONTACT WITH THE JUDGE

When answering questions asked by either attorney, address your answers to the judge, while you maintain good eye contact with him. Good body language and eye contact will reinforce the truthfulness and rightfulness of your position. You want to maintain "good" eye contact. Don't "stare down" the judge or jury!

BRING ALL NEEDED DOCUMENTS AND THINGS TO COURT

You should have previously provided your attorney with all of the documents and things that he or the opposing attorney have requested. As a precaution, bring all of the relevant documents and things in your possession, and tell your lawyer what you have brought.

DO WHAT IS BEST FOR YOUR CHILDREN, THEN DO WHAT IS BEST FOR YOU. HOPEFULLY THEY ARE THE SAME.

CONCLUSION

Now that you have reviewed all of the insights found here, you have the significant advantage of being informed and prepared. You are equipped with the ability to work with your attorney to reach the most advantageous outcome. You have the ability to control your emotions and financial security. You have minimized the chance that your spouse can take advantage of you. One of the most dramatic messages found here is that you are not alone. In the time that it took you to read this book, thousands more have divorced and resolved issues of child custody, visitation and child support. The great distinction between you and the literal millions who have ventured these perilous times is that you are prepared for the test. Additionally, if you desire further assistance, the author is available for your inquiries.

THE ULITMATE FAMILY LAW RECOMMENDATION

Become prepared and knowledgeable!

Best Wishes!

Stephen Rue

Attorney at Law

APPENDIX

LOUISIANA COURTHOUSE MAILING ADDRESSES
(in alphabetical order by parish)

Acadia Parish Clerk of Court "P.O. Box 922 "Crowley, LA 70527
Phone: (337) 788-8881

Allen Parish Clerk of Court "P.O. Box 248"Oberlin, LA 70655
Phone: (337) 639-2030

Ascension Parish Clerk of Court " P.O. Box 192 "
Donaldsonville, LA 70346
Phone: (985) 473-9866

Assumption Parish Clerk of Court " P.O. Drawer 249 "
Napoleonville, LA 70390
Phone: (985) 369-6653

Avoyelles Parish Clerk of Court " P.O.Box 196 "Marksville, LA 71351
Phone: (318) 253-7523

Beauregard Parish Clerk of Court " P.O.Box 100 " DeRidder, LA 70634
Phone: (337) 463-8595

Bienville Parish Clerk of Court " 100 Courthouse Drive, Room 100 " Arcadia, LA 71001
Phone: (318) 263-2123

Bossier Parish Clerk of Court "P.O. Box 430 " Benton, LA 71006
Phone (318) 965-2336

Caddo Parish Clerk of Court " 501 Texas Street, Room 103 "
Shreveport, LA 71101
Phone: (318) 226-6780

Calcasieu Parish Clerk of Court " P.O. Box 1030 " Lake Charles, LA 70602
Phone: (337) 437-3350

Caldwell Parish Clerk of Court ¨ P.O. Box 1327 ¨ Colombia, LA 71418
Phone: (318) 649-2272

Cameron Parish Clerk of Court ¨ P.O. Box 549 ¨ Cameron, LA 70631
Phone: (337) 775-5316

Catahoula Parish Clerk of Court ¨ P.O. Box 198 ¨ Harrisonburg, LA 71340
Phone: (318) 744-5497

Claiborne Parish Clerk of Court ¨ P.O. Box 330 ¨ Homer, LA 71040
Phone: (318) 927-9601

Concordia Parish Clerk of Court ¨ P.O. Box 790 ¨Vidalia, LA 71373
Phone: (318) 336-4204

De Soto Parish Clerk of Court ¨ P.O. Box 1206 ¨ Mansfield, LA 71052
Phone: (318) 872-3110

East Baton Rouge Parish Clerk of Court ¨ P.O. Box 1991 ¨ Baton Rouge, LA 70821
Phone: (225) 389-3960

East Carroll Parish Clerk of Court ¨ 400 First Street ¨ Lake Providence, LA 71254
Phone: (318) 559-2399

East Feliciana Parish Clerk of Court ¨ P.O. Box 559 ¨ Clinton, LA 70722
Phone: (225) 683-5145

Evangeline Parish Clerk of Court ¨ P.O. Drawer 347 ¨ Ville Platte, LA 70586
Phone: (337) 363-5671

Franklin Parish Clerk of Court ¨ P.O. Box 431 ¨ Winnsboro, LA 71295
Phone: (318) 435-5133

Grant Parish Clerk of Court ¨ P.O. Box 263 ¨ Colfax, LA 71417
Phone: (318) 627-3246

Iberia Parish Clerk of Court ¨P.O. Box 12010 ¨New Iberia, LA 70560
Phone: (337) 365-7282

Iberville Parish Clerk of Court ¨ P.O. Box 423 ¨ Plaquemine, LA 70764
Phone: (225) 687-5160

Jackson Parish Clerk of Court ¨ P.O. Box 370 ¨ Jonesboro, LA 71251
Phone: (318) 259-2424

Jefferson Parish Clerk of Court ¨ 800 Second Street ¨ Gretna, LA 70053
Phone: (504) 364-2900

Jefferson Davis Parish Clerk of Court ¨ P.O. Box 799 ¨ Jennings, LA 70546
Phone: (337) 824-1160

Lafayette Parish Clerk of Court ¨ P.O. Box 2009 ¨ Lafayette, LA 70502
Phone: (337) 233-0150

Lafourche Parish Clerk of Court ¨ P.O. Box 818 ¨ Thibodaux, LA 70302
Phone: (985) 447-4841

La Salle Parish Clerk of Court ¨ P.O. Box 1372 ¨ Jena, LA 71342
Phone: (318) 992-2158

Lincoln Parish Clerk of Court ¨ P.O. Box 924 ¨ Ruston, LA 71270
Phone: (318) 251-5130

Livingston Parish Clerk of Court ¨ P.O. Box 1150 ¨ Livingston, LA 70754
Phone: (225) 686-2216

Madison Parish Clerk of Court ¨ P.O. Box 1710 ¨ Tallulah, LA 71282
Phone: (318) 574-0655

Morehouse Parish Clerk of Court ¨ P.O. Box 1543 ¨ Bastrop, LA 71220
Phone: (318) 281-3343

Natchitoches Parish Clerk of Court ¨ P.O. Box 476 ¨
Natchitoches, LA 71457
Phone: (318) 352-9321

Orleans Parish Clerk of Civil District Court ¨401 Loyola
Avenue¨New Orleans, LA 70112
Phone: (504) 592-9104

Ouachita Parish Clerk of Court ¨ P.O. Box 1862 ¨ Monroe, LA
71210
Phone: (318) 327-1444

Plaquemines Parish Clerk of Court ¨ P.O. Box 129 ¨ Pointe-a-
la-Hache, LA 70082
Phone: (985)333-4377

Pointe Coupee Parish Clerk of Court ¨ P.O. Box 86 ¨ New
Roads, LA 70760
Phone: (985) 638-9596

Rapides Parish Clerk of Court ¨ P.O. Box 952 ¨ Alexandria,
LA 71309
Phone: (318) 473-8153

Red River Parish Clerk of Court ¨ P.O. Box 485 ¨ Coushatta,
LA 71019
Phone: (318) 932-6741

Richland Parish Clerk of Court ¨ P.O. Box 119 ¨ Rayville, LA
71269
Phone: (318) 728-4171

Sabine Parish Clerk of Court ¨ P.O. Box 419 ¨ Many, LA
71449
Phone: (318) 256-6223

Saint Bernard Parish Clerk of Court ¨ P.O. Box 1746 ¨
Chalmette, LA 70044
Phone: (985) 271-3434

Saint Charles Parish Clerk of Court ¨ P.O. Box 424 ¨
Hahnville, LA 70057
Phone: (985) 783-6632

Saint Helena Parish Clerk of Court ¨P.O. Box 308
¨Greensburg, LA 70441
Phone: (985) 222-4514

Saint James Parish Clerk of Court ¨ P.O. Box 63 ¨ Convent, LA 70723
Phone: (985) 562-7496

Saint John the Baptist Parish Clerk of Court ¨ P.O. Box 280 ¨ Edgard, LA 70049
Phone: (985) 497-3331

Saint Landry Parish Clerk of Court ¨ P.O. Box 750 ¨ Opelousas, LA 70570
Phone: (337) 942-5606

Saint Martin Parish Clerk of Court ¨ P.O. Box 308 ¨ St. Martinville, LA 70582
Phone: (337) 394-2210

St. Mary Parish Clerk of Court ¨ P.O. Drawer 1231 ¨ Franklin, LA 70538
Phone: (337) 828-4100 ext. 200

Saint Tammany Parish Clerk of Court ¨ P.O. Box 1090 ¨ Covington, LA 70434
Phone: (985) 898-2430

Tangipahoa Parish Clerk of Court ¨ P.O. Box 667 ¨ Amite, LA 70422
Phone: (985) 549-1610

Tensas Parish Clerk of Court ¨ P.O. Box 78 ¨ St. Joseph, LA 71366
Phone: (318) 766-3921

Terrebonne Parish Clerk of Court ¨ P.O. Box 1569 ¨ Houma, LA 70361
Phone: (985) 868-5660

Union Parish Clerk of Court ¨ Courthouse Building ¨ Farmerville, LA 71241
Phone: (318) 368-3055

Vermilion Parish Clerk of Court ¨ P.O. Box 790 ¨ Abbeville, LA 70510
Phone: (337) 898-1992

Vernon Parish Clerk of Court ¨ P.O. Box 40 ¨ Leesville, LA 71496
Phone: (318) 238-1384

Washington Parish Clerk of Court ¨ P.O. Box 607 ¨
Franklinton, LA 70438
Phone: (985) 839-7821

Webster Parish Clerk of Court ¨ P.O. Box 370 ¨ Minden, LA
71058
Phone: (318) 371-0366

West Baton Rouge Parish Clerk of Court ¨ P.O. Box 107 ¨
Port Allen, LA 70767
Phone: (985) 383-0378

West Carroll Parish Clerk of Court ¨ P.O. Box 1078 ¨ Oak
Grove, LA 71263
Phone: (318) 428-2369

West Feliciana Parish Clerk of Court ¨ P.O. Box 1843 ¨ St.
Francisville, LA 70775
Phone: (985) 635-3794

Winn Parish Clerk of Court ¨ P.O. Box 137 ¨ Winnfield, LA
71483
Phone: (318) 628-3515

DISCLAIMER

This guide is not intended or offered as advice for legal, medical or physiological problems. Please consult a licensed attorney, health care provider, counselor, and/or religious advisor for real legal, medical, psychological, and/or spiritual needs. This book does not provide legal advice. The content is merely concepts to be discussed with your attorney. Every effort was made to present accurate information. The publisher and the author assume no liability associated for any errors and/or omissions. Consult your attorney as to the applicability and accuracy of the contents presented in this book.

ABOUT THE AUTHOR STEPHEN RUE; TO CONSULT WITH THE AUTHOR AS A LOUISIANA DIVORCE, CHILD CUSTODY AND CHILD SUPPORT ATTORNEY

The author, Stephen Rue is an experienced and respected attorney who represents clients with family law issues of divorce, child custody and child support and other matter. Stephen is a graduate of Southern Methodist University in Dallas, Texas where he received a Bachelor in Business Administration degree. He also has received two post-graduate degrees from Loyola University — a law degree and an MBA. He also completed fellowships at The National Institute of Trial Advocacy and The Institute of Politics.

Since university, Stephen has become one of the most high profile divorce attorneys in New Orleans. He is a regular lecturer at seminars and classes for attorneys and law students throughout the country.

Stephen Rue has litigated well over 1,000 divorces. Stephen's notable cases include filing the first petition in Louisiana history seeking a sexually abused child's "divorce" of his father. He also litigated one of Louisiana's first "Baby Jessica" styled paternity/custody cases. Additionally, Stephen represented the mother in a custody battle after her children attempted to poison her. Stephen is aggressive in his pursuit for the rights of parents and their children.

Stephen is a familiar attorney who has been interviewed on television and radio stations throughout Louisiana. He is routinely consulted as a legal advisor for some of these stations.

Stephen Rue has been voted the "Best Attorney" (in 2013) and "Best Divorce Lawyer" (in 2002 and 2003) in New Orleans by GambitWeekly's yearly readers' poll. Stephen Rue has previously served as the Vice-Chairman of the Civil Law and Litigation Section of the Louisiana State Bar Association.

Stephen Rue is the senior attorney at Stephen Rue & Associates, a law firm that represents persons throughout Louisiana, with greater focus in representing clients in Orleans (New Orleans), Jefferson, St. Tammany, St. Charles, St. John the Baptist, St. Bernard and Plaquemines Parishes. For further information about author/attorney Stephen Rue or to make an appointment with a divorce lawyer, call (504) 529-5000.

Contact Attorney Stephen Rue through his website or email address:

Web Site and E-Mail:

www.RueDivorce.com

StephenRue@me.com

(504) 529-5000

CPSIA information can be obtained
at www.ICGtesting.com
Printed in the USA
LVOW04s2149171116
513480LV00014B/580/P

9 781499 300710